DR

Is God Enough for You?

Lessons on Conquering Temptation

HYLES PUBLICATIONS • HAMMOND, INDIANA
www.hylespublications.com

COPYRIGHT © 2005
Hyles Publications

1st Printing – March 2005
2nd Printing – March 2008

ISBN: 0-9764247-4-6

All Scripture quotations are from the King James Bible.

All rights reserved. If you would like to print any portion of this book, please contact Hyles Publications for written permission.

CREDITS
Project Manager: Dr. Bob Marshall
Assistants: Rochelle Chalifoux and Kristi Wertz
Transcription: Barbara Burke
Page Design and Layout: Linda Stubblefield
Proofreading: Rena Fish, Julie Richter

To order additional books by Dr. Jack Schaap,
please contact:
HYLES PUBLICATIONS
523 Sibley Street
Hammond, Indiana 46320
www.hylespublications.com
e-mail: info@hylespublications.com

Dedication

It has been my privilege here at First Baptist Church of Hammond to minister to hundreds of precious souls who have struggled with addictions of all kinds through our faith-based addiction ministry, Reformers Unanimous. What a profound impact this ministry is having on the lives of those who have faced indescribable temptations and who struggle with many of those temptations on a daily basis.

Due to the personal and powerful leadership of Brother Chris Tefft and his outstanding volunteer staff at Reformers Unanimous, victory is now a daily reality in the lives of those who formerly were enslaved by dangerous and demeaning addiction.

I dedicate this book to Brother Chris Tefft and his excellent workers at Reformers Unanimous. Thank you for the superb ministry you provide and the Christian love you demonstrate in word and in deed.

I owe a great debt of gratitude to my editorial advisor, Mr. Mike Fish, who has labored long and hard to make my thoughts and heart clear to my readers. Since 1983, Brother Fish has been an employee of Hyles-Anderson College in various capacities. He presently serves there as the director of public relations, and he teaches part-time on the faculty. He has worked in the bus ministry in various positions since 1984, and he has been a Sunday school teacher since 1990.

"Moreover, brethren, I would not that ye should be ignorant, how that all our fathers were under the cloud, and all passed through the sea; And were all baptized unto Moses in the cloud and in the sea; And did all eat the same spiritual meat; And did all drink the same spiritual drink: for they drank of that spiritual Rock that followed them: and that Rock was Christ. But with many of them God was not well pleased: for they were overthrown in the wilderness. Now these things were our examples, to the intent we should not lust after evil things, as they also lusted. Neither be ye idolaters, as were some of them; as it is written, The people sat down to eat and drink, and rose up to play. Neither let us commit fornication, as some of them committed, and fell in one day three and twenty thousand. Neither let us tempt Christ, as some of them also tempted, and were destroyed of serpents. Neither murmur ye, as some of them also murmured, and were destroyed of the destroyer. Now all these things happened unto them for ensamples: and they are written for our admonition, upon whom the ends of the world are come. Wherefore let him that thinketh he standeth take heed lest he fall. There hath no such temptation taken you but such as is common to man: but God is faithful, who will not suffer you to be tempted above that ye are able; but will with the temptation also make a way to escape, that ye may be able to bear it. Wherefore, my dearly beloved, flee from idolatry. I speak as to wise men; judge ye what I say."

(I Corinthians 10:1-15)

Table of Contents

Chapter One
 How to Escape Temptation 9

Chapter Two
 Opening Myself to Temptation 19

Chapter Three
 The Root Cause of Temptation 33

Chapter Four
 The Source of Temptation 47

Chapter Five
 The Path of Temptation 65

Chapter Six
 The Great Distraction 85

Chapter Seven
 I Understand It, But I Don't Get It! 103

CHAPTER ONE

How to Escape Temptation

I am of the opinion that the best way to escape temptation is to avoid being tempted. Logically, if one Christian is tempted half as many times as another Christian, the first will probably succumb to temptation half as many times as the other.

My life is built on the premise that I don't know if I am strong enough to handle all the temptations that come my way, and I don't want to find out. Therefore, I have built for myself a lifestyle that prevents me from being tempted. I cannot keep away from all temptation—that is impossible. I have within me a sinning nature that is prone to wander. I cannot eliminate all temptation; however, the less I am tempted, the less likely I am to yield to temptation.

> "When a Christian isolates himself as an exception, he becomes vulnerable to temptation."

If Christians would stop enjoying the temptation process, they would cease the sin process. Many Christians don't want to sin, but they enjoy flirting with sin. To avoid sin, the Christian must avoid temptation. The Christian needs to stay many steps away from sinful activity, so that, should he stumble and fall, the fall may take him into temptation but not into sin. I believe it is best to avoid temptation altogether.

There are several things we must understand to avoid temptation:

10 ❧ Is God Enough for You?

1. Ignorance is the number one reason for yielding to temptation. I Corinthians 10:1 says, "*Moreover, brethren, I would not that ye should be ignorant....*" Ignorance does not mean "I didn't know." The word *ignorance* means "to ignore." If I ignore someone, I am acting ignorant. The word *ignorant* has been misused to describe someone who is not very smart. However, the word *ignorant* in the Bible is used to mean a person who is ignoring something he does know or should know. Therefore, ignorance is not the same thing as unlearned. If somebody is ignorant scripturally, it means that he knows better but is ignoring what he knows; or, he is of age and should know better, but he is ignoring what is common knowledge.

When a person ignores the obvious, he gets into trouble. For example, a man is rushed to the hospital with a massive heart attack. The doctor says, "Have you had any symptoms?"

The patient says, "Oh, for about six weeks now, I have had this tremendous pressure on my chest and tingling and numbness in my left arm. I've had a little trouble breathing and severe chest pain. What do you think it is, Doc?" That patient ignored all the obvious symptoms. To ignore the symptoms is to beg the consequences.

The whole thrust of I Corinthians 10 is four-fold: First, how to avoid temptation; second, how not to become a casualty; third, how not to get into trouble with the Lord; and fourth, how not to fall. God gives us warning signs to avoid temptation.

One of our staff ladies returned her lease car to the lease company at the end of the lease. The agent noticed there was black tape on the dashboard. When he peeled off the tape, the red oil light was on. He mentioned to the staff lady, "I noticed there was black tape on the dashboard."

She said, "Oh, yes. A red light came on, and it would not go out. It bothered me so badly I finally covered it with a piece of

How to Escape Temptation

tape." He called the shop and drained the crankcase. There was only ½ cup of oil in the motor! It was a miracle that the engine didn't seize up or crack a piston or a cylinder. That light was there as a warning light. God gives us many "warning lights" to avoid temptation. When a person ignores the "warning lights of temptation," he is bound to suffer the consequences.

"When a person ignores the 'warning lights of temptation,' he is bound to suffer the consequences."

2. **No one is an exception to temptation.** When a Christian believes he is an exception, he is more susceptible to temptation. I Corinthians 10:1-4 uses the word *all*. All of these people had something in common. All of these people had many experiences together, but some of them thought they were exceptions to the rules. A Christian opens himself to temptation the moment he starts saying, "But you don't understand what I have to live with. But you don't understand my circumstances. But you don't have my past." The moment the Christian isolates himself from the crowd, he opens himself up to possibilities for temptation.

Notice these phrases in I Corinthians 10:1-4: *"were all baptized," "did eat all the same spiritual meat," "did all drink the same spiritual drink."* As long as they were all together, they had strength. However, the moment one of them separated himself from the unit, he became an isolated person open to temptation. This isolated person is the young man who separates himself from the school procedures. He is the one who says, "I don't want to be like all those goody-two-shoes—all those people trying to please the authorities." Every Christian should be like the right crowd. If all the kids in school are doing right, then every kid should be with "the all."

Thomas became a doubter because he wasn't with all the other disciples. If he had been with the other disciples, he would

Is God Enough for You?

have been present when Jesus appeared to them. When a person doesn't want to run with the good crowd and isolates himself for whatever reasons, he falls victim to temptation.

> *"So much is said to teenagers and children about not running with the wrong crowd that we sometimes forget that there is a good crowd with whom to run."*

When a person is trying to build a fire on a grill, he will start with several charcoal briquettes. He lights them and gets them all hot, and they turn white hot as long as they are together. However, if one of those coals is moved by itself on the grill, it will quickly cool off. People who stray from those who are "hot" for righteousness will find themselves "cool" to the things of God.

Similarly, one who strays from those who are doing right is like a pioneer who would refuse to circle his wagon with the wagon train. In pioneer days, when the Indians were attacking the wagon train, the people would circle the wagons and pull together and build a defense. If one wagon owner had said, "No, I'll fight the Indians myself," the rest of the people would have buried his dead body the next morning.

The book of Judges describes a group of people who did not follow the good crowd. *"Every man did that which was right in his own eyes."* (Judges 21:25) Judges is filled with perversion. It has stories that I am afraid for little children to read. There was no one pulling the people of God together; therefore, they pulled apart and each did his own thing. They were morally massacred.

Christians are naturally different from each other in looks, stature, hair color, tastes, eye color, appetites; however, when it comes to right and wrong, we are all supposed to be the same. But the moment a person uses his background or circumstances to say, "I'm an exception; you don't understand how I was reared," he is advertising his availability for temptation.

How to Escape Temptation

A person becomes susceptible to the lure of temptation the moment he says, "I would become what I'm supposed to become, but you don't know what I had to live with." Each person should decide that what he had to live with is what made him what he is and that his circumstances are pleasing to God. The truth of the matter is that too many people are looking for an excuse to hide behind their weakness.

Let's follow the logic of the person who says, "I grew up in the city where gang graffiti was everywhere. Where I grew up, there were problems like prostitution and immorality and ungodliness and liquor and drug dealers and people getting shot. That's why I sin, because I grew up in a sinful environment." Okay, then why did Adam and Eve sin? What graffiti was sprayed on their trees? Nobody cut them off in traffic. Nobody offered them drugs or liquor. With every excuse we give for why we sin, there is a Bible story that proves our excuse to be fallacious. As long as we want to hide behind our environment, our parents, or our background, we will never gain the victory over temptation. People are looking for an excuse in case they do wrong so they will be able to say, "That's why I did it."

> "*Once a person feels that he is an exception to particular rules, he is advertising that he is available for temptation.*"

3. Believers all share common ground. I Corinthians 10:1-4 lists five things that all Christians share. In understanding these five things, a Christian builds a safety net around himself as protection from temptation.

A. *We are all under the protective care of our Heavenly Father.* We are all *"under the cloud."* That cloud was the visible presence of Jehovah God. That cloud was not just a tiny pillar. The crowd of people was as large as the number of residents in the city of Chicago—about three million. That's a very big pillar of cloud!

14 — Is God Enough for You?

By daytime, the cloud shaded the people from the heat of a 135° desert. At nighttime, it turned into a fire and gently warmed them from the 35-45° nighttime temperatures. The pillar was a visible sign that God cared for His people.

The rebel children of God left the will of God many times, but they never left God's care. Those who were rebellious still enjoyed the cooling effect of the cloud by day and the warmth of the fire by night. They all had the same protection of the same Heavenly Father. Every Christian has the same God with mercies and grace for all.

The moment a Christian decides that God cares about others more than He does for him, that Christian has just advertised that he is available for temptation. As long as I believe that I am protected like any other Christian is, then I have no more right to sin than anyone else.

A Christian may be tempted to say, "But God's been that Christian's Father longer than he has been my Father." One son cannot be more of a son than another son. That my sister is five years older than I does not make her more of a family member than I am. Are newborns less a family member than the older children in a family? Christians sometimes use nonsense logic. We all have the same Heavenly Father with the same protection of God.

B. *We all were delivered the same way.* I Corinthians 10:1 says that they **all** passed through the sea. The entire Hebrew nation crossed the Red Sea. Archaeologists find no reason why the Red Sea is called the Red Sea. I'll tell you why: the Red Sea represents the blood of Jesus Christ. Everyone gets saved the same way—by grace through faith. How do bus kids get saved? By grace through faith. How do college educated people get saved? By grace through faith. How do homeless people get saved? By grace through faith. How do women get saved? By grace through faith.

How to Escape Temptation   15

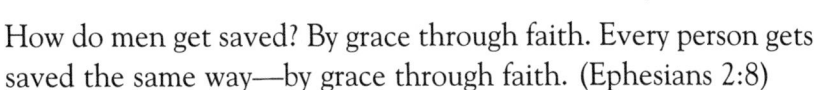

How do men get saved? By grace through faith. Every person gets saved the same way—by grace through faith. (Ephesians 2:8)

For a Christian to separate himself from the crowd and say he is an exception to the rules is to say, "I probably got saved differently than you did, too." The Bible says, *"Neither is there salvation in any other: for there is none other name under heaven given among men, whereby we must be saved."* (Acts 4:12) Jesus said, *"I am the way, the truth, and the life: no man cometh unto the Father, but by me."* (John 14:6) If all people get saved in the same way, then what gives one person the right to look at the dirty magazines when the rest cannot? Why can one listen to rock 'n' roll music and the other cannot? There is only one Heavenly Father who saves "whosoever will" the same way.

God says that when a Christian ignores the fact that every sinner is saved the same way, he is advertising his availability to temptation. Temptation is shut down when a Christian says, "I have the same Heavenly Father watching over me as everyone else does."

C. *We all follow the same spiritual leader, Christ.* I Corinthians 10:2 talks of the Israelites' leader Moses. Hebrews tells us that Moses was a type of Christ. As the Israelites went through the Red Sea, they were following Moses. The picture was so powerful. The Jews were following Moses, a type of Christ, and walking through the Red Sea, a type of salvation that Christ provided.

If I have the same spiritual leader as you have, and I have been delivered the same way that you have been delivered, and I have the same Heavenly Father watching over me as you have watching over you, then neither of us has an excuse to sin in our thought life or to sin in our actions or to sin in our marriage or to sin on our job or to sin in our other relationships. The same Heavenly Father Who is watching us misbehave is also watching our neighbor.

16 Is God Enough for You?

The reason a person sins is because he chooses to ignore the fact that every Christian has the same Heavenly Father Who is watching, Who saves the same way, and Who has provided the same spiritual leader, Jesus Christ.

D. *We all have the same spiritual food (I Corinthians 10:3).* Those people in the Old Testament had to pick up off the ground a sweet wafer called manna. It was lying on the ground every morning. They would gather it and then sometimes make meal out of it and bake it. The majority of those people had no idea what they were eating (*manna* means "What is this?" [Exodus 16:15]). They were eating angels' food. (Psalm 78:24-25)

Christians today have comparable spiritual food—the Word of God. A Christian is tempted when he ignores the spiritual manna—the same spiritual food as that of which strong, victorious Christians are partaking.

When I was growing up, we had horses, and we also boarded other people's horses. My job was to feed the horses and clean the stalls. All the horses were given the same food—oats, bran, and hay. Once in a while, if we were trying to fatten up the horses for the wintertime, we gave them corn. Feeding them bran gave them a nice, shiny coat. The horses received a lot of high-protein energy when we fed them oats. All of the horses received the same meal. Not one of the horses ever said to me, "I don't want oats today. I'll have filet mignon."

When a Christian wants to eat his own diet, he opens himself to temptation. Mission men need to "eat" the Bible. College students need to "eat" the Bible. Nursing home residents need to "eat" the Bible. College professors need to "eat" the Bible. Students need to "eat" the Bible. High school kids need to "eat" the Bible. Staff members need to "eat" the Bible. Choir members need to "eat" the Bible. Musicians need to "eat" the Bible. All Christians need to "eat" the same spiritual food. If we do, we will

How to Escape Temptation

all have the same spiritual strength to withstand the same spiritual temptations.

Job 23:12b says, "*I have esteemed the words of his mouth more than my necessary food.*" Job decided to read the Bible at least as often as he ate food. If Christians would decide to do as Job did, it would help them against their temptations.

A Christian may say, "I don't understand the Bible." A person does not have to understand all the ingredients in his food for those ingredients to have an effect on him. A Christian does not have to understand all the finer points of the Bible for it to effect his life.

I believe the King James Version is the preserved Word of God. Most Christians don't understand all the controversy over the issue of which Bible is the correct one. One reason I believe the King James Bible is the Word of God is the effect it has on people. First Baptist Church has hundreds of people saved every week using the King James Bible. If you believe the New International Version is the right one, show me your converts. If you believe the Revised Standard Version is the right one, show me your Sunday school kids who have changed lives. If you believe the New American Standard Version is the right one, show me your bus routes. The funny thing is, I have been to some of these so-called super-mega churches filled with a bunch of rich people. I have yet to see their buses or their homeless ministries or their rescue missions. They just want a social club, and they brag about having three or four baptized each month. Bless God! We had 383 people baptized one Sunday alone. On another Sunday, we had 1,084 people walk an aisle trusting Christ. I **know** the King James Bible works!

E. *We all drink the same spiritual drink—Christ.* If Christ is good enough for salvation, He is good enough for every other part of the Christian's life. If church is good enough for a Christian on

18 ❧ Is God Enough for You?

Sunday morning, why not Sunday night and Wednesday night?

I do not understand this business of "Christ is good enough to take me to Heaven, but not good enough to run my family" or "Christ is good enough for my salvation, but not good enough for my finances." I want Christ to be good enough for every area of my life. I want to build my marriage on Christ. I want to rear my children on Christ. "On Christ the Solid Rock I stand. All other ground is sinking sand."

> *"There is no secular organization that can satisfy the Christian like the local church."*

"Wherefore let him that thinketh he standeth take heed lest he fall. I speak as to wise men; judge ye what I say." (I Corinthians 10:12, 15) A group is stronger than a single man. The force of a group can handle an attack better than the strength of one solitary life!

Many groups and organizations can satisfy the need for acceptance, but it is the local church that God started and purchased with His blood (Acts 20:28) that can help the Christian be strong and remain consistent in his battles with temptation.

CHAPTER TWO

Opening Myself to Temptation

The best way to escape temptation is to avoid being tempted. If I am tempted half as much as someone else, I will probably yield to temptation half as much as that person. If I don't want to sin at all, I had better learn how to not be tempted.

The problem with so much of Christianity is that good people who do not want to sin enjoy the journey up to the door of sin. They enjoy the titillation. A Christian will never be what God intends for him to be until he not only despises the sin but also despises the journey that leads to the sin. A person cannot get in his automobile and head to the station of sin and say, "I'm just going to stop a little short of it; but I'm going to have a good time on the journey." That attitude reveals a wicked heart.

> "*Every appetite is an invitation saying, 'I'm open to temptation.'*"

Interstate 94 connects Chicago, Illinois, and Detroit, Michigan. Suppose a person gets off the exit to go to Chicago and I ask him where he is going, and suppose he says, "I'm going to Detroit." No matter what he says, if he is pointed in the wrong direction he will not make it to his destination. If a Christian gets off the exit that says "Sin and Destruction," the Christian may say, "I'm going to stop at the city limits"; but when he gets into the traffic on that highway, he will not be stopping short of the city limits. He will end up right in the middle, and the crowd will pull him along. By the time a Christian realizes he is approaching the station of sin, it is too late to put on the brakes because he is caught up in the momentum of the temptation. A Christian needs to back up to the exit and say, "I don't even want to look at the exit."

The Bible lays out for us in I Corinthians how we tempt ourselves and how we become tempted Christians. First, as I stated in the previous chapter, we isolate ourselves from common ground. There is strength in unity. The devil then starts telling the weak Christian that he doesn't fit in with the righteous crowd. The ones who isolate themselves are the ones who get in trouble.

When a Christian isolates himself as an exception, he becomes vulnerable to temptation. If in any area of a Christian's life he feels that he is an exception, he is saying, "Here I am. Hit me, Devil."

I Corinthians 10:13 says, *"There hath no temptation taken you but such as is common to man...."* There has never been a temptation that has faced a Christian that many other Christians have not faced also. The Bible says in Hebrews 4:15, *"For we have not an high priest which cannot be touched with the feeling of our infirmities; but was in all points tempted like as we are, yet without sin."* The pastor may not know how a person feels, but the Lord Jesus knows exactly how each person feels and can identify with the feelings and emotions of each.

Jesus knew what it was like to grow up in a stepchild situation. Jesus knew what it was like not to be accepted by his brothers and sisters. Jesus knew rejection. Jesus knew what it was like to be personally tempted by Satan. Yet, Jesus never said, "You don't know what it's like to be the Son of God. You don't know how much pressure it is to be God."

Opening Myself to Temptation

There are several ways a Christian opens himself up to temptation and being tempted. If he can avoid these areas, he can be successful in avoiding temptation.

1. A Christian opens himself to temptation because he has *undisciplined appetites*. God gives us several negative examples of undisciplined appetites in I Corinthians 10 so that we can learn from the mistakes of others. Notice in verse 6, *"Now these things were our examples, to the intent we should not lust after evil things, as they also lusted."* The more self-discipline a Christian has, the more unlikely he is to be a victim of temptation.

Samson was a victim of temptation. He was a Spirit-filled young man, but he habitually put himself in the way of temptation. His vulnerability to temptation was his unbridled lust (appetite) for women. Samson could not say "No" to a pretty girl. He associated with women of the Philistines. He was also going after other heathen women. He went after a harlot even though he knew she was a harlot. That undisciplined appetite opened up an unholy door of temptation.

King David is another example of a man having unbridled appetites. There was a time each year when kings would go fight battles. David should have been fighting a battle, but he remained at home.

> *"It is a dangerous thing to have a man of passion bored."*

He was walking around his house with nothing to do. It is a dangerous thing to have a man of passion bored. He should have been out killing giants but instead was looking for something to do. The Devil always makes sure that the unoccupied Christian finds something to do. David found her—Bath-sheba.

All appetites that a Christian has need to be brought under subjection to the Spirit of God. James 1:14-15 says that we sin when we are drawn away of our own lusts. Every appetite is an invitation saying, "I'm open to temptation." So, we must bridle those appetites and be very careful. Temptation is simply an opportunity to sin. I want to be unaware of the opportunity to sin.

When my dad used horses on the farm, he often put blinders on the horses if they were plowing near a road or taking a hay wagon down the road. The horse could see just a very narrow strip in front of him. This would keep the horse from being distracted by sudden flashes of light or a moving vehicle or something shiny or another animal or a child. That sudden light or noise or movement could frighten a horse, and he might bolt.

I wish we could put some spiritual blinders on teenage boys and girls. I wish we could put some moral blinders on college young people. I wish we could just point them in the right direction and say, "There is graduation day" and then focus their sight so that they could see nothing but graduation day in front of them. Instead, their eyes are roving back and forth.

Christians know too much about sin. As a pastor, I labor in prayer agonizing to try to get Christians to cut their ties from the world. Christians need to shut off their televisions. Christians need to stop listening to **all** the news. We don't need to be **that** informed, especially when we can do nothing about what we hear. The news just makes us aware of how rotten, sick, sad, and sinful this old world is. Christians need to put on their spiritual blinders and read the Word of God.

I was talking to a man recently who was struggling with his business. He was putting in long hours and just not succeeding. I said, "Can I tell you what Russell Anderson and Jack DeCoster, both millionaires in their given fields, and other godly successful businessmen have told me about their successes? Russell Anderson told me personally that he studies the Bible two hours every morning. Jack DeCoster never spends less than one and one-half hours a day (and most of the time spends two to two and one-half hours a day) in his Bible. Jack DeCoster said, 'I want

Opening Myself to Temptation

God to be real to me.' " No wonder he is the largest egg producer in the entire world! These men have discovered the great secret—that success is found in the Word of God. They have put on spiritual blinders and concentrated their focus on reading the good news in the Word of God.

I asked Brother DeCoster, "How much television do you watch?"

He said, "I don't have time for television. I don't play. All I do is walk with God and work."

> *"Any appetite that is out of control is a breeding ground for temptation."*

Men who want to succeed at something should get in the Book a couple of hours every morning. They should put some spiritual blinders on their eyes and stop looking at the Internet and the television shows.

Having unsatisfied desires and undisciplined appetites provides a haven for opportunities to sin, which are a breeding ground for temptation. Eli's undisciplined appetites destroyed his sons. In refusing to restrain himself, he also refused to restrain his children.

There are certain sins that today's Christianity says are okay. Any appetite that is out of control is a breeding ground for temptation. Some parents have trouble with their children because they, the parents, have undisciplined appetites. Dads who are on the Internet looking at sexy lingerie ads and other such things have a tough time cracking the whip on their sons. Parents are so distracted by their own sins that they do not have the time to help their children with their sins.

Again and again, I have had a wife sit in my office for counseling and she will say, "If I could get my husband off the Internet and away from the pornography, my son would stop messing around with the girls." Proverbs 26:2 says, "...*the curse causeless shall not come.*" There is always a reason for things that go bad. I don't point fingers at people who are hurting or who are having a tough time. I believe each individual is a free moral agent. I believe an adult child can make his own decisions and can break his parents' hearts. However, the Bible says that when a person has an undisciplined appetite—whether monetary, physical, material, sexual—he is inviting sin to come in.

2. A Christian opens himself to temptation by idolatry. I Corinthians 10:7, *"Neither be ye idolaters, as were some of them; as it is written, The people sat down to eat and drink, and rose up to play."* Nothing is wrong with eating and drinking and playing **unless** those activities are the primary focus in life, for self. I Corinthians 10:31, *"Whether therefore ye eat, or drink, or whatsoever ye do, do all to the glory of God."*

The word *idolatry* means "any activity in which a Christian does not bring glory to God." I'm so glad that I am married to a spiritual woman. We were chatting one day about Cheez-its, her favorite snack. She ordered, "Get those away from me."

"Why?" I asked. "You can eat those."

She said, "I don't think that pleases the Lord when I indulge in those."

"Aw!"

> *"If a Christian will make his eating and drinking glorify God, then maybe the other areas of life will fall in line quite naturally."*

She said, "Don't 'aw' me. The Bible says that whether we eat or drink, do all to the glory of God." I hate it when my wife goes to preaching! I get convicted. Thank God there's no altar in our house because I'd be walking the aisle often!

I walked away thinking that if she is concerned about whether eating Cheez-its brings glory to God, then I guess I don't have to worry about her committing adultery. I guess I don't have to worry about what she's watching on television. If a Christian will make his eating and drinking glorify God, then maybe the

Opening Myself to Temptation

other areas of life will fall in line quite naturally. I thank God I am married to a disciplined woman.

Idolatry is any activity that does not bring glory to God. Next time you watch television, could you invite the Lord Jesus to sit down and say, "Lord, this R-rated program will bring pleasure to You." Do you think Jesus, sitting beside you, would find pleasure in watching people acting like animals on the television screen? Was Jesus Christ honored by what you watched on television last night?

Teenagers who go on activities, is Jesus honored by your behavior? College students, is Jesus Christ honored and magnified by your dating? Man or lady in the office, is Jesus honored by your office behavior?

It is time we have a baptism of holiness in our children. And just as important, we need a baptism of holiness in the parents of our children! It is time we have a baptism of Christians saying, "God, I don't want to leave that crowd of righteous people."

The way a Christian listens in church ought to bring pleasure to Jesus Christ. The way a Christian drives a car ought to bring glory to Jesus Christ. The Christian's home, his activities, and his humor ought to bring glory to Jesus Christ.

Leaders must never pull their followers aside from the righteous crowd and say, "Let me tell you some humor that would not be appropriate over there." Leaders who do so are setting their followers up for temptation, and they are setting them up by saying that there are areas of life that do not have to be in submission to Jesus Christ.

Idolatry is anything pulled out of the "all" of I Corinthians 10:31. Idolatry says, "**That** does not have to fit under the category of righteousness."

A leader may tell a follower, "Why don't you come to my house, and we'll watch some videos? A bunch of us are getting

26 ❧ Is God Enough for You?

together to watch a video. It's R-rated, but there's nothing really bad in it. There's one scene that's bad, but I'll tell you when it's coming up, so you don't have to watch it. There is swearing in it, but not too much."

> *"Every time a Christian separates a segment of his life from all that is right to do, he becomes a vulnerable target."*

Should adults ever wonder why a really good kid gets in trouble? Those young people who are allowed by authorities or their peers to pull a part of their life away from glorifying God become a vulnerable target for the tempter to nail them smackdab between the eyeballs. Others who would never use bad language or bad humor or watch a racy video may skip church to go to a ball game. Every time a Christian separates a segment of his life from all that is right to do, he becomes a vulnerable target.

In Numbers 11:1-3, the people who got burned the most in the camp of the Israelites were those who lived on the fringe. Moses lived in the middle of the camp. Moses was the one who wrote in Psalm 91, *"He that dwelleth in the secret place of the most High shall abide under the shadow of the Almighty. I will say of the LORD, He is my refuge and my fortress: my God; in him will I trust. Surely he shall deliver thee from the snare of the fowler, and from the noisome pestilence. He shall cover thee with his feathers, and under his wings shalt thou trust: his truth shall be thy shield and buckler. Thou shalt not be afraid for the terror by night; nor for the arrow that flieth by day."*

If a Christian gets back in the middle of the camp, he will find himself under the shadow of the Almighty, and when the Devil launches his arrows at him, they will fall short. The same arrows make direct hits upon those who live on the fringe of the will of God.

Those who want to live on the edge are right in range of the

Opening Myself to Temptation

Devil. Those who want to live on the edge with their music and their videos and their morality are going to get hit by the arrows of the tempter because those people are no match for Satan.

However, those who live right smack-dab in the middle under the shadow of mom and dad, under the shadow of the local church, under the shadow of the Word of God, under the shadow of the old-time Gospel songs, under the shadow of righteousness, under the shadow of old-fashioned standards and convictions, under the shadow of decency and respect for authority, and under the shadow of right are protected.

Woe be to the leadership that pulls people out of the middle. Woe be to those leaders who say, "There are rules you have to keep, and then there are rules that are just put in the rulebook, but are not intended to be enforced."

> "**B**ad information about sexuality has fostered an immoral situation in our Bible-believing churches."

Most of the entertainment that many Christians have is of no value to righteousness or to the glory to God. It's time Christians drew a line and said, "Let's get in or get out! Let's decide we are going to be in this thing called real, live, sincere Christianity with no double standards." I am tired of double standards, and I am sure God is also!

3. A Christian opens himself to temptation through fornication. I Corinthians 10:8 says, *"Neither let us commit fornication, as some of them committed, and fell in one day three and twenty thousand."*

From the time that I can remember, sexuality has been misrepresented, mistaught, and misunderstood. Bad information about sexuality has fostered an immoral situation in our Bible-believing churches. Sex is not a bad word. Romantic love between a husband and wife is not a bad thing. It is a gift from God. God said, *"Marriage is honourable in all, and the bed undefiled:*

28　Is God Enough for You?

but whoremongers and adulterers God will judge." (Hebrews 13:4a)

However, romantic love is as sacred as the Lord's Supper, and God says that we must be careful how we handle it. The Lord's Supper is so sacred that if a Christian mishandles it, God might kill him. (I Corinthians 11:29, 30) God does not want Christians joking about the Lord's Supper because it represents the body and the blood of Jesus Christ. It represents how a person gets saved. Symbolism in the New Testament is extremely important. When church members are partaking of the Lord's Supper and kids tease and laugh about it, they are tempting Almighty God to kill them. It is not a laughing matter; it is extremely serious. However, although the Lord's Supper is sacred and blessed, we **can** talk about it. God said that some people have abused it and made it a means of salvation; that practice is prostituting and defiling the Lord's Supper. The Lord's Supper is a picture of the grace of God.

> "When a Christian commits fornication, he is acting out a symbol that says, 'Christ is not the only Saviour.' "

In I Corinthians 10:8, we learn that some people in the Old Testament misunderstood sexuality, and God killed 23,000 in one day and another 1,000 the next day. A group of 24,000 people died because they said, "We don't understand what sexuality is." It is not a dirty thing. It is so sacred that God tells us to reserve it for marriage.

When a Christian commits fornication, he is acting out a symbol that says, "Christ is not the only Saviour." That's why God hates sexual sins so badly. When an unmarried couple mess around and fondle each other like a married couple is allowed to do and should be doing, they are saying, "There are other Saviours besides Christ." Human sexuality between a husband and wife is reserved for a man who represents the Lord Jesus Christ as Saviour and a woman who represents the Bride of

Opening Myself to Temptation

Christ, the local church. When a couple takes liberties outside the bonds of marriage, they are saying, "A person doesn't have to get saved to go to Heaven." They are symbolizing that it is okay for a person to choose his own way to Heaven.

Salvation is a commitment to Christ. Marriage is a man representing Christ saying, "I receive you as my bride," and the bride of Christ, the individual believer, who says, "I receive you, Christ, as the **only** groom for me." Jesus said, *"I am the way, the truth, and the life: no man cometh unto the Father, but by me."* (John 14:6b) Fornication is acting out polytheism and more than one way to Heaven.

> *"We need some sex education in the homes where parents tell their children that sex is a man and a woman who are married acting out how intimate God and the believer should be."*

We need some sex education in the homes where parents tell their children that sex is a man and a woman *who are married* acting out how intimate God and the believer should be. When an unmarried couple commits fornication, they are violating everything for which the Bible stands. That's why no sin in the Bible is punished more than sexual crimes.

There is only one time in the Bible that a man was turned over to Satan for the destruction of the flesh. He was a man in I Corinthians 5 who was committing a sexual sin. Paul said, "If that boy doesn't stop that sexual violation, I have permission from God to pray for God to turn him over to Satan for the destruction of the flesh."

Young people who are messing around sexually are pulling away from the righteous crowd and saying, "God, hit me! Satan, hit me!" That attitude is foolishness! God can hit pretty hard.

4. A Christian opens himself to temptation by tempting Christ. I Corinthians 10:9 says, *"Neither let us tempt Christ, as* some of them also tempted, and were destroyed of serpents."

Exodus 17:2, 7 says, "Wherefore the people did chide with Moses, and said, Give us water that we may drink. And Moses said unto them, Why chide ye with me? wherefore do ye tempt the LORD? And he called the name of the place Massah, and Meribah, because of the chiding of the children of Israel, and because they tempted the LORD, saying, Is the LORD among us, or not?"

What does it mean to tempt Christ? Let me share some examples.

- A student believes he undeservedly gets in trouble at school and says, "Sometimes I wonder whose side God is on anyway."
- A couple wants to have a baby and says, "What are You doing up there, God?"
- A college student says, "I got punished, and I don't deserve it. Sometimes I think God has it in for me."
- An employee says, "So-and-so got a raise at work, and I didn't get a raise. God, where are You when I need You?"
- A married couple having marital challenges say independently of each other to God, "God, this mate You gave me is not what I bargained for!"

Christians better be careful when they start charging God foolishly and accusing Him of not watching over them. They had better get back in the middle of the crowd and say, "God sure is good, isn't He? Finances are bad, but God is still good. My wife and I aren't getting along very well, but God is still good. My kids are having a tough time in school, but God is still good."

God does not have much patience with those who want to tell Him how to run the universe. Job tried that, and in essence God said to Job, "Where were you when I laid the foundations of Heaven? Where were you when the morningstars sang at the founding of the world? Did you make leviathan? Do you know where wisdom came from? Do you know what makes a sparrow fly? Do you know how a snowflake is designed? Job, I was there before you came. I'll be there when you are gone! I am God Almighty! Don't stick your finger in My face!"

The moment a Christian thinks that God is not fair, the Devil is there to walk up and put his arm around the Christian and say, "You sure have it tough. God sure makes life tough for you." While Satan is talking, he is telling his henchmen, "Draw in close. Get the arrows. Pierce his heart." Satan watches Christians tumble and says, "Suckers!"

5. A Christian opens himself to temptation by murmuring. I Corinthians 10:10 says, *"Neither murmur ye, as some of them also murmured, and were destroyed of the destroyer."* When Christians complain and gripe and whine, God turns them over to the destroyer. The best defense against temptation is praise and gratitude.

CHAPTER THREE

The Root Cause of Temptation

"James, a servant of God and of the Lord Jesus Christ, to the twelve tribes which are scattered abroad, greeting. My brethren, count it all joy when ye fall into divers temptations; Knowing this, that the trying of your faith worketh patience. But let patience have her perfect work, that ye may be perfect and entire, wanting nothing. If any of you lack wisdom, let him ask of God, that giveth to all men liberally, and upbraideth not; and it shall be given him. But let him ask in faith, nothing wavering. For he that wavereth is like a wave of the sea driven with the wind and tossed. For let not that man think that he shall receive any thing of the Lord. A double minded man is unstable in all his ways. Let the brother of low degree rejoice in that he is exalted: But the rich, in that he is made low: because as the flower of the grass he shall pass away. For the sun is no sooner risen with a burning heat, but it withereth the grass, and the flower thereof falleth, and the grace of the fashion of it perisheth: so also shall the rich man fade away in his ways. Blessed is the man that endureth temptation: for when he is tried, he shall receive the crown of life, which the Lord hath promised to them that love him. Let no man say when he is tempted, I

> "Testing is an opportunity to prove that there is nothing I need outside of what God provides, and each test purges me of those appetites which tell me I need more."

34 ❧ Is God Enough for You?

am tempted of God: for God cannot be tempted with evil, neither tempteth he any man: But every man is tempted, when he is drawn away of his own lust, and enticed. That when lust hath conceived, it bringeth forth sin: and sin, when it is finished, bringeth forth death. Do not err, my beloved brethren." (James 1:1-16)

James chapter 1 gives a marvelous practical teaching about the root cause of temptation. In the Garden of Eden, man made a moral choice which was the wrong choice. There were two choices man could have made in the garden, and man chose the wrong one. In making the choices, man was confronted with two trees: a tree of knowledge of good and evil and a tree of life. Man chose to "eat" knowledge rather than to partake of life.

"When a Christian is tempted, it is an attempt by God to provide once again the test man should have passed in the Garden of Eden."

Humans would rather live a life of unhappiness and know what is going on in everybody else's life than to live a life of righteousness and happiness and be fairly ignorant. Though man was redeemed at the cross, Christian mankind is on a constant journey to reclaim what was lost in the Garden of Eden. Christians face habitual and regular opportunities called temptations. The word *temptation* is the word "adventure, opportunity, attempt." It does not mean, by itself, a seduction to do evil.

Notice the word *"trying"* in James 1:3, *"the **trying** of your faith worketh patience."* The same word is used in James 1:12, *"Blessed is the man that endureth temptation: for when he is **tried**...."* God gives us opportunities to go back and make "Garden-of-Eden" decisions again.

When a Christian faces temptation, he must understand that there is no sin in being tempted. Temptation is not sin. When a Christian is tempted, it is an attempt by God to provide once

The Root Cause of Temptation

again the test man should have passed in the Garden of Eden.

The Bible tells the Christian not to run from temptation but to ask God to deliver him from evil. However, every opportunity to stand for right is an opportunity to go back, figuratively, to the Garden of Eden and say, "I'm reclaiming what was lost there. I want life." Every temptation is a Christian's opportunity to prove or to be tested and to reclaim what was lost by Adam's actions in the Garden of Eden.

To understand this truth, several statements about testing are helpful to comprehend:

1. Each test is an opportunity to prove that there is nothing I need outside of what God provides. All temptation provides for me an opportunity to make a resounding, thundering statement that says, "Christ is all I need." God has provided me with everything I want.

James 1:4 says, *"But let patience have her perfect work, that ye may be perfect and entire, wanting nothing."* The proof of the test is that I have need of nothing. If I successfully pass the temptation and can walk away from temptation, by doing so I am saying, "See, I don't need what was offered. What I need is what I already have."

While a Christian is walking the journey of the Christian life, he comes to a temptation. He can say, "This is an opportunity for me to show that back in the Garden of Eden, Adam blew it; but I'm going to try to reclaim what he lost. I don't need the sinful choice. What I need is what I already have, and what I have is God."

A young college man who has lived a somewhat sheltered life may be tempted to see what he has been missing all of his life. He may have been brought up as a little Sunday school boy and is innocent and pure and clean and decent. Then, in a moment of weakness, glittering lights and seductive women pull at his heart.

36 ❧ Is God Enough for You?

He may even stop at a "gentlemen's club" to see what it's like. While he is there, he is bombarded with feelings and emotions and is overwhelmed with what he is seeing and hearing. Then he has to live with the guilt of "I wonder if my family will find out?"

Then the young man falls in love with a pure young lady, and he knows in his mind that he cheated on her. He did not necessarily do anything with the wicked women, but he soiled his conscience and spoiled the fabric of his soul morally. When he marries, he carries that stain with him. One day temptation comes. Maybe he and his wife are not getting along very well, or maybe she is sick and the romance is weak. The temptation comes, and he thinks that maybe he can find a satisfaction outside of what God has provided with his wife. In his mind and heart, he has opened a door that says to God, "You and what You provide are not sufficient for me."

A teenager may be tempted to try illicit drugs—maybe marijuana. He has smelled it and wondered about its effects. So, he opens the door of temptation and buys some marijuana cigarettes. The effects he experiences may not be what he expected, but then he does it again and again. He becomes very weak to that temptation; so, when the opportunity comes to choose life or to choose what he knows, he chooses what he knows instead of life. In so doing, he is saying to God, "What You are and what You provide for me are not sufficient."

> "Every time the Christian succumbs to the sinful option of temptation, he figuratively points his finger at God and says, 'You're not enough for me!' "

Every time the Christian succumbs to the sinful option of temptation, he figuratively points his finger at God and says, "You're not enough for me!" The beauty of not yielding to temptation is that every time the Christian faces temptation and walks away from it, he is saying, "God, **You are** enough for me." When

The Root Cause of Temptation

a Christian is satisfied with God and what God has provided for him, then the temptation to seduction and evil has no power over him.

If I am content with my wife, then nobody else can get me. I do not want anybody else because I am content with what I have. The moment a husband becomes discontented with his wife, it is not a failure on his wife's side; it is the husband's deciding to evaluate what God has provided and to judge His gift. The Bible says, *"And a prudent wife is from the* LORD*"* (Proverbs 19:14b) and *"Whoso findeth a wife findeth a good thing, and obtaineth favour of the* LORD*."* (Proverbs 18:22) If a husband (or a wife) wants somebody else, that desire is insulting the spouse, and it is also insulting God and saying, "What **You** provided me is not adequate."

God gives each Christian the same choice He gave Adam and Eve. Each can choose the tree of life and live totally satisfied forever, or he can choose the tree of knowledge and never be satisfied again. Whether it is a child's temptation to take a piece of candy at the grocery store when mama's not there and the clerk is not looking, or a teenager's temptation to smoke a cigarette or to look at a dirty magazine or listen to rock music, that temptation is an opportunity for him to resist the temptation and say, "God, what I have from You is sufficient."

2. Each test purges me of those appetites that tell me I need more. Inside the Christian are lusts and appetites that are a constant reminder to cause the Christian to desire more. Every time a Christian says "No" to temptation and wrong, he purges himself of that need to have what would not satisfy him if he had it.

If pornography satisfied like a wife does, why wouldn't a man just buy one issue? If a man chooses one wife and chooses to stay with her and chooses to find all his joy in her, then he will not need even one magazine or one Internet chat room or one "gentlemen's" club. The men who go to "gentlemen's" clubs return over and over again because they are never satisfied. Men who buy one pornographic magazine buy more and more magazines because those women do not satisfy. Once a Christian opens the door that leads to knowledge, that knowledge never satisfies. He never knows enough.

I am very satisfied with one woman. Young people who make the choice to stay pure and to keep themselves for one person have no idea how happy and satisfied they will be on their wedding day. Conversely, the couple who decides to reach out and indulge in a physical relationship because "After all, we love each other, and we're going to get married; so let's go ahead and sample our sexuality." Those couples find dissatisfaction all the way through their marriage. A Christian who says "No" to temptation finds a satisfaction. The Christian who says "Yes" to temptation finds dissatisfaction.

Every time a Christian says "No" to marijuana, he is saying "I'm satisfied with what I have." Every time a Christian says "Yes" to marijuana or illegal drugs, he will never be satisfied. If cigarettes satisfy, why do people have "three-packs-a-day" habits? Because once a person says "Yes" to temptation, there begins an insatiable desire for more and more.

As with most happy and content people, I have found my satisfaction with one wife. I have found my satisfaction with one church. I have found my satisfaction with one Bible. I have found my satisfaction with one Gospel. I have found my satisfaction with one Christ. I have found my satisfaction with the truth. I do not need all the "other" because the "other" never satisfies.

Testing is an opportunity to prove that there is nothing I need outside of what God provides, and each test purges me of those appetites that tell me I need more.

3. The byproduct of the test is wisdom. When a Christian survives a test, he steps into the zone of increased wisdom. People

The Root Cause of Temptation

ask me how to get wisdom. Wisdom is attained by continuing to say "No" to the temptations that produce sinful appetites.

Every time a Christian gives in to another temptation, he increases his foolishness. A Christian gets rid of the foolishness in himself by doing right. Wise people "see" better. Wise people say, "Trust me on this. You'll never be satisfied with marijuana because it will take you to cocaine, which will not satisfy you and will lead you to another drug."

The root cause of all temptation was found in the Garden of Eden. God gave Adam dominion over everything. God gave Adam a wife and everything he needed. But Adam said "Yes" to the temptation of knowledge, and every man since Adam has fought the feelings of dissatisfaction for what God provided in his life.

Some couples say, "We're not happy because we don't have children." The question should be asked of such dissatisfied couples: "How many children did Adam and Eve have before the temptation?" Zero. Children are usually a byproduct of satisfied people who do not need children. Some people who have children in order to make up for a lack in their lives have a hard time letting go of their children when they get older. All kinds of problems come when a person is looking for something else to give satisfaction—something other than God.

How many possessions did Adam and Eve have? They had nothing materially speaking. They had God. God gave them food. God gave them each other. God wanted them to be satisfied with what He gave them. Anything a person acquires beyond what God gives him is an opportunity to see that the things we desire do not satisfy after all.

An unfaithful spouse cannot tell about the affair he had and how it satisfied him. When he tires of that relationship, then he will seek another. The person who has one pornographic magazine is never satisfied with one. Those men usually have hundreds of magazines stashed away in boxes because one never satisfies.

Every time a Christian opens the door to temptation, he is opening a door that says, "I need more. I need more," and that appetite destroys the Christian. The serpent said to Adam and Eve, "God is trying to deprive you of something that He alone has, and He doesn't want you to have." If Adam and Eve would have said, "We have God. We have each other. That's all we need," they sure would have been happy. They would have chosen life instead of knowledge.

The Christian who says, "I want to know if there is something more for me. I want to know if there's a thrill at a 'gentlemen's' club. I want to know if there's excitement in having an extramarital affair. I want to know if there is fulfillment in pornography. I want to know if there is excitement in liquor. I want to know if there is fun in drugs," will find damnation, abomination, and an appetite that never goes away! The only satisfaction is in saying "No" to temptation!

The crutch of Jesus Christ is the best crutch on which a Christian will ever lean. The crutch of the Word of God is the best crutch on which a Christian will ever lean. A test is an opportunity to prove that there is nothing a Christian needs outside of what God provides for him. Each test purges the Christian of those appetites that tell him he needs more. The byproduct of each successfully passed test is increased wisdom.

4. God cannot be tested to reveal what He lacks. The Bible says, *"for God cannot be tempted with evil."* (James 1:13b) Man can never prove to God that He needs something else. God is totally content with or without humanity. The Christian will never find satisfaction until he comes into God's arena. There is nothing we can offer God that He would want beyond what He is.

How ludicrous to believe that a human could offer God any-

The Root Cause of Temptation

thing that would make God a more complete God! The test is to say that everything God has is available to the Christian. If God is totally satisfied with what He is, then how can the Christian find satisfaction apart from what God has?

When a Christian gives in to temptation, he is saying, "God, I bet You are as dissatisfied with being God as I am with me." God needs nothing. Jesus and God and the Holy Ghost were very happy with each other before there ever was a man. God did not make man because He was dissatisfied. God did not put a Garden of Eden on Earth because He was dissatisfied. God did not say, "I'm an unhappy God. Jesus, I'm tired of you. I want something more. I want man." No! God said, "We're so happy, why don't we let some others enjoy this happiness? We're so content with each other; let's give this enjoyment to others."

God made mankind to enjoy the contentment that the Godhead has known from eternity past before time could be measured. Every time a Christian gives in to temptation, he is saying, "I believe You are a dissatisfied God, aren't You?" God is a very content God.

A young couple asked me as their pastor to pray that they would have a child. I anointed them with oil. They returned months later, still with no child. I anointed them again, but still they had no child. The third time they returned, and once again I anointed them with oil. Several months passed, and I received a note from the couple saying, "We're expecting our child."

I said, "I'm not surprised." When that couple returned the second and third times, I asked them, "What if God does not give you a baby?"

The husband looked at his wife, reached across the table and took her hand, and said, "I've got my baby right here."

I said, "As long as that's where you are, I don't mind praying for you. If I have to pray and you have to lean on me to give you something that God has not provided, I'll probably lose you as church members."

The seed bed of dissatisfaction, whether for a noble thing like a child or for a pay raise or a nicer car or a bigger house or a vacation in the Bahamas or whatever it is a person feels he has to have to make him happy, is exactly the soil from which temptation sprouts. If a couple says, "We're not happy. We've got to have babies. If God doesn't give us babies, we're going to be mad at God," they may as well say, "We want an affair, and we want to be anointed with oil that God would give us an affair." That is the same kind of foolish thinking. If, in order to be happy, a Christian has to have something that God has not provided, then he is opening the door to be tempted by all sorts of evil.

> "*If*, in order to be happy, a Christian has to have something that God has not provided, then he is opening the door to be tempted by all sorts of evil."

If a single person says, "If God doesn't give me a mate in the next six months, I'm going to ditch church. I'm going to get out of religion. I'm going to live the way I want to live!" that person has a spiritual problem. When a person cannot get to the point where what he is is what he needs and what he has is what he wants and God is all he needs, then temptation will open the door to "I want. I want. I want." And the person will never be satisfied.

If a Christian cannot be satisfied with the King James Bible, cannot be satisfied with old-fashioned preaching, cannot be satisfied with convictions and standards, cannot be satisfied with the music of the choir, then, no doubt, he will find it difficult to be satisfied in any area of his life!

Teenagers will often say, "There's music for church, but then I have **my** music." If church music does not satisfy the members,

The Root Cause of Temptation

then they are opening themselves up to a world that will cause all kinds of hurt. The dissatisfied Christian is saying, "The old songs of Heaven aren't good enough for me."

Christians become seduced when they think they need something beyond what God supplies. In the Garden when Satan said, "Yea, hath God said?" Adam and Eve should have said, "Yes, He did! Shut up and get out of here!" Instead, by their actions they said, "What do you mean?" Satan then convinced them that God was holding back something that was good for them. If God is withholding something from a Christian, it is only to enrich that Christian's life and make him a better person. *"No good thing will he withhold from them that walk uprightly."* (Psalm 84:11c)

> **"If** God is withholding something from a Christian, it is only to enrich that Christian's life and make him a better person."

Some Christians want things from God so badly that they have to be careful that they do not get dissatisfied when that for which they ask doesn't come fast enough. I am very intense in my prayer life. I was praying in my office one Saturday night, and I got on my knees and said, "God, I'm going to ask you for some big miracles. Here are the things I want." Then I listed four things. That Sunday morning all four things happened! Praise God! I was on shouting ground all afternoon.

But that Saturday night after I had asked God for those four things, the Spirit of God smote my heart and said, "Jack, just in case I don't do those things for you, how are you going to feel about it?"

I told God, "I read a verse this morning that said, *'I will greatly praise the* LORD *with my mouth.'* (Psalm 109:30a) That verse prompted me to take the next several minutes and praise God specifically. I have a great Book! I have a great salvation! I have

44 🙢 Is God Enough for You?

a great wife and great kids! I have a great church! I have a great job! I have a great Holy Ghost! I have a great house in which to live. I have a great wardrobe. I have a great car to drive to church! I live in a great state! I live in a great country! I have a great President! God, I have great deacons, a great staff, great musicians, and a great choir. I have such a great God!"

God said, "Better go to church. I have something special for you."

When Christians believe that what they have is great, God doesn't mind giving them what they want, because God knows that if they do not get what they want they will still be happy with the great things they already have. The problem that most Christians have is to *minimize* what they have and *maximize* what they don't have. They begin thinking "I have a small God. I have a mealy-mouthed wife. I attend a so-so church. I have an okay Book. I live in a menial country. I have an alright salvation." The reason some members leave churches is because they never magnified how good it was to be a part of a great church. Instead, they minimize and fault-find and criticize.

> "*The problem that most Christians have is to minimize what they have and maximize what they don't have.*"

When a Christian stops magnifying what he **does not** have, stops minimizing what he **does** have, and starts magnifying what he **does** have, he shuts the door on temptation. It is like going back to the Garden of Eden and choosing life that God gives instead of knowledge of something unknown.

If one chooses life, then he gains wisdom and more wisdom and more wisdom, and he learns God and becomes so content. Look at the faces of those older people who have stayed faithful to each other like the Lee Robersons. They are so happy. Ask Dr. Lee Roberson, pastor for over 40 years at the great Highland Park

The Root Cause of Temptation

Baptist Church of Chattanooga, Tennessee, how many pornographic magazines it takes to make him happy. Zero! He has had one woman who has made him happy all those years. He chose life and happiness.

The root cause of all temptation goes all the way back to the Garden of Eden. The Christian wants to magnify what he doesn't have and minimize what he does have. In so doing, he will lose what he does have and forfeit what he doesn't have. He will lose it all. The tree of life is the best choice. Choose life. Say "No" to temptation.

CHAPTER FOUR

The Source of Temptation

"Then was Jesus led up of the spirit into the wilderness to be tempted of the devil. And when he had fasted forty days and forty nights, he was afterward an hungred. And when the tempter came to him, he said, If thou be the Son of God, command that these stones be made bread. But he answered and said, It is written, Man shall not live by bread alone, but by every word that proceedeth out of the mouth of God. Then the devil taketh him up into the holy city, and setteth him on a pinnacle of the temple, And saith unto him, If thou be the Son of God, cast thyself down: for it is written, He shall give his angels charge concerning thee: and in their hands they shall bear thee up, lest at any time thou dash thy foot against a stone. Jesus said unto him, It is written again, Thou shalt not tempt the Lord thy God. Again, the devil taketh him up into an exceeding high mountain, and sheweth him all the kingdoms of the world, and the glory of them; And saith unto him, All these things will I give thee, if thou wilt fall down and worship me. Then saith Jesus unto him, Get thee hence, Satan: for it is written, Thou shalt worship the Lord thy God, and him only shalt thou serve. Then the devil leaveth him, and, behold, angels came and ministered unto him." (Matthew 4:1-11)

> "Multiple choosing is what gets Christians into trouble. In man's use of the power to choose, he will ultimately abuse the power to choose and thus self-destruct."

48 — Is God Enough for You?

It is crucial that the Christian understand the subject of being tempted and falling victim to temptation. Temptation is a major work of the Devil. Satan is trying to get the Christian to stumble and to fall and bring shame and reproach to the cause of Christ.

When King David stumbled terribly in II Samuel chapter 11, his sinning with Bath-sheba led to his ordering the murder of her husband. Nathan the prophet went to King David and told him an incredible story about a rich man who owned hundreds of sheep and lived next door to a poor man who had one little lamb. The lamb was a family pet and even slept with the family. When the rich man had a visitor, he told his servants to go get the pet lamb next door for a meal and not to take any of his own flock. As Nathan told David the story, David became very angry and said that the man that did that was going to die, and he would pay back fourfold. (II Samuel 12:5-6) Nathan confronted the king with the words, "...*Thou art the man....*" (II Samuel 12:7)

David was face-to-face with his succumbing to temptation and sin. Nathan said that David had given the enemies of God great occasion to blaspheme. When the Christian falls victim to temptation, the results are not just about him. The results are first and foremost about the Lord Jesus Christ and His work and His kingdom. The words "slip up," "stumble," or "fall" are less condemning words to describe when a Christian sins overtly and purposely and with wicked intentions of his own accord. That Christian gives the enemies of God great occasion to criticize and blaspheme God.

When a church member does some thoughtless deed and his church's name gets in the newspaper, he makes the church congregation look like they have a black eye. His sin brings shame on a lot of good people. The church does not treat sinners with great grace so that they can get strong enough to go sin again. The church tries to get the sinner strong enough so that he does not

The Source of Temptation

fall victim to that sin again and so he will stay far away from that sin. When a sinner gets saved, great glory is brought to the Lord Jesus Christ. Much damage is caused if a sinner goes back into the same vile lifestyle he had before he was saved.

Those who sin are not people who are not smart; those who sin are smart people who did not think they would ever get into sin. Certainly many ideas exist regarding the source of temptation. Very simply, I believe the source of temptation lies in man's ability to choose.

> *"Those who sin are not people who are not smart; those who sin are smart people who did not think they would ever get into sin."*

1. **Before sin entered into the world, Adam was given a great power—the power of choice.** Genesis 2:19, 20 says, *"And out of the ground the LORD God formed every beast of the field, and every fowl of the air; and brought them unto Adam to see what he would call them: and whatsoever Adam called every living creature, that was the name thereof. And Adam gave names to all cattle, and to the fowl of the air, and to every beast of the field; but for Adam there was not found an help meet for him."* According to these verses, God gave Adam a tremendous power to make choices, and God kept Adam's choices. God did not undo Adam's choosing. As the animals came by, Adam said, "We'll call that an anteater," and God agreed.

Adam said, "Call that next one a camel."

Adam continued naming all the animals, and whatever label Adam chose, God accepted. I believe that Adam was the most brilliant creation God ever made. He had an incredible mind and was untainted and undefiled by sin. God gave Adam the power to make the choice, and He conceded to whatever choice Adam made. God gave Adam the power to choose, but Adam had to live with his choices; however, God also had to live with Adam's choices.

2. Having the power to choose tempts us to choose simply because we can. I believe the greatest power that God has given to mankind is the power to choose. Individuals may choose to get saved when they read a Gospel tract or hear a salvation message. They also have the choice to crumple up the Gospel tract or ignore the salvation message.

The power to choose tempts us to want to use the power often. Having power can be likened to having a Corvette in the garage. On the first sunny day, the top goes down, and the Corvette comes out of the garage; the tires get squealed, and rubber gets burned. There is no fun having power if you do not use it. I love speed. I used to race dirt bikes, and my motto was, "The faster you can go, the better." I'm sure many thought I would kill myself! When I used to fly airplanes, I did trick flying. I figured if you've got it, you want to flaunt it.

> "God gave us a great power in the power of choice, and when we choose, God Himself abides with our choices."

God gave us a great power in the power of choice, and when we choose, God Himself abides with our choices. The continual temptation man faces is to use that great power again and again and again and "to lay choice marks" all over the "streets" of his life.

The Bible says, *"But as the days of Noe were, so shall also the coming of the Son of man be."* (Matthew 24:37) They were buying and selling and marrying and giving in marriage. (Matthew 24:38) People often ask me the meaning of that verse and what is wrong with buying and selling and marrying and giving in marriage. There is nothing wrong with those actions. Those actions represent people making choices. I believe the Lord is saying that people will always be exercising the power to choose. The problem is that people will not be exercising the power to choose in the right manner. Jesus was saying, "They'll be

The Source of Temptation

buying and selling and marrying and giving in marriage, but they will not be using their tremendous power to evangelize the world." There will be such an absence of faithful people spreading the faith because people will be using the great power of choice for themselves—buying and selling and marrying and giving in marriage.

3. The power of choice is the greatest power given to man. Angels had one choice. The Bible seems to indicate that the angels of old had one choice, and when they made that one choice, their choosing was done. In Jude verse 6 the Bible says, *"And the angels which kept not their first estate, but left their own habitation, he hath reserved in everlasting chains under darkness unto the judgment of the great day."*

There was a day when angels had a choice: whether to follow God or the rebellion of Lucifer. The Bible indicates in Revelation chapter 12 that one-third of the angels chose to follow Lucifer, and two-thirds of the angels decided to follow God. The angels who chose to follow Lucifer became the demons we read about in the Gospels. Those devils and demons cannot undo that decision.

When the demoniac of Gadara who had a legion of devils inside his body was confronted by Jesus, the devils ran to Jesus and worshipped and said, *"What have I do do with thee, Jesus, thou Son of the most high God?"* (Mark 5:7) The devils know Who God is. The devils said, "Don't send us out into the darkness." Jesus sent them into some pigs instead. Those demons had made a choice many years before, and their choice was incontrovertible.

When Jesus died on the cross, He did not die for the devils. Every devil could look to the cross and know that Jesus was the Son of God dying. They knew He was redeeming. They knew Jesus had the power to save. However, none of Jesus' efforts were for the devils because they had made an unchangeable choice. But man has the power to make multiple choices.

4. **The power to choose is the most abused power given to man.** With the knowledge that man has the power of choice, it is apparent Satan tempts man with multiple choices. The temptation of Jesus Christ in Matthew chapter four was not a singular temptation. Jesus was tempted of the Devil forty days. Three of those unique temptations are listed in chapter four: one from a pinnacle where the Devil suggested that Jesus jump off and that the angels would rescue him; another time the Devil suggested that Jesus turn stones into bread (Jesus had been fasting forty days). Lastly, Jesus was shown all the kingdoms of the world. Satan told Jesus that if He would fall down and worship him, Jesus would be given all the kingdoms.

One of the great temptations in this chapter was the temptation to choose. What would have been so bad about Jesus turning the stones into bread to feed Himself? He would have been making a choice that was not His to make. What would have been wrong with Jesus' jumping off the pinnacle and letting the angels catch Him? After all, the Bible says in Psalm 91:11-12 that God would give the angels charge over Jesus. He would have been making a choice when it was not time to make a choice. It was not time for Jesus to decide if He wanted the kingdoms. He would get those later on when He would be crowned King of kings and Lord of lords. Multiple choosing is what gets Christians into trouble. In mankind's use of the power to choose, he will ultimately abuse the power to choose and thus self-destruct.

5. **If temptation is simply the opportunity to sin, then the power to choose is the most dangerous power to have.** Oftentimes, people who love the Lord, love the Bible, and love the church are free and easy and loose and careless with their choices and get themselves into trouble. They are making choices they should not make because they are simply exercising their power to choose.

The Source of Temptation

Multiple opportunities plus multiple choices equals eventual bad choices—every time. People who have made bad choices are consistently making further bad choices. It is a marvel that people who make terrible choices and say, "We made a bad choice. What do we do?" They usually reply, "I don't want to do **that**. **This** is what I want to do" when they are told what to do. That person got in trouble in the first place by using his "chooser." If he would shut off his "chooser" for a few minutes and let somebody else choose for him, he would stop making dumb choices.

> **"Multiple opportunities plus multiple choices equals eventual bad choices—every time."**

Single ladies in our church who want their wedding on our church platform better be virgin when they walk on the platform. If they want to wear a white gown, then they should be clean and pure. They should be an innocent, sweet representation of the wedding gown they put on. The platform of a church should not be trashed because a woman made a bad choice. She still wants everything she would have received had she not made that bad choice. She could have a nice wedding in a chapel or a small ceremony in a pastor's office; however, the platform of a church is for those who made wise choices. If a girl is carrying an illegitimate baby, she has forfeited the privilege of the honor of wearing a white wedding gown which signifies purity and chastity.

For all young girls who go forward in church and say that they are going to be pure until their wedding day, there is a special prize for doing right. That prize is to have a big church wedding with all of their family and church friends and the honor of wearing a white gown. Likewise, the man should stand on the platform as a pure, innocent young man right with God, right with his future in-laws, right with his mom and dad, and reserved for his bride to be.

54 ❧ Is God Enough for You?

The church's kindness should not be abused by people who choose to make self-destructive choices. Those who choose to be fornicators and whoremongers and adulterers ought not have all the rights and privileges pertaining to those who have remained pure for such a special ceremony. They ought not! They do have forgiveness. They should have the love and prayers of their pastor. God knows that those kids who get in trouble and those people who mess up before their marriages need the prayers of those who love them, but their choices have caused them to forfeit certain privileges.

There was a day when people who committed an immoral sin were ashamed. People must understand that if they make bad choices, they must stop insisting that their "chooser" is adequate or on par with the "chooser" of the pastor or other wise authorities.

Young people who choose to be holy and pure have used their "chooser" wisely. When Adam said, "Hippopotamus, rhinoceros, camel," God said, "Okay." When Adam said, "Fruit," God said, "Now I get to choose. Get out of the Garden." Just moments before, God had let Adam choose the names of all the animals, and God had accepted Adam's choices. However, how Adam and Eve chose to behave in God's Garden gave God the choice to expel them from the Garden.

God killed a lamb and took the skin to cover Adam and Eve. When Adam saw something die for the first time, Adam realized that his choice to interfere with God's choices had huge repercussions. Adam's seeing the death of the animal was only a small portion of the consequences of his sin. If Adam had looked ahead 4,000 years, he would have seen the Son of God hanging on a cross.

If people think that I am hard on sin, they have never been to Calvary. If people think that I have an obstinate, opinionated,

The Source of Temptation

hard-headed attitude toward sin, they have never been to my Saviour's cross! They have never seen Christ butchered on the cross! At the cross is the place where we find out what God really thinks about sin.

People who make bad choices consistently make further bad choices. They must put down **their** "chooser" and stop pulling the trigger of choice and saying, "Choice, choice, choice; that's what I want to do." They need to put down their "chooser" and let somebody else make some choices for them. People get into trouble when they use the power of choice too much.

> *"At the cross is the place where we find out what God really thinks about sin."*

I believe that Jesus' temptation was that of multiple opportunities to make personal choices. Satan gave Jesus alternative options to make decisions apart from the will of God. Jesus stayed true to principles and would not allow His flesh to decide.

When a student's life gets out of rhythm (such as at the end of a school year), he gets out of schedule. He makes choices about watching television and playing video games and going to the beach. Even some teachers, staff members, and employees seem to forget that God works on a 12-month calendar and not a school calendar. They go through the inane, stupid, naive, foolish system of starting to choose whether they should stay at First Baptist Church or leave. They come to my office and say, "Should I stay or leave?" Who told them they had to choose? Someone please give me the Scripture verse that tells school employees that they must choose in May whether they are going to stay or leave.

Where is the verse that college students must decide each year whether they are going to return to college or not? They need to put down that broken "chooser." They chose to attend college several years before; and by choosing to attend college, they should have chosen to graduate. That was a free choice, and that choice doesn't need to be made ever again! One may say, "I have a big opportunity. If I go home for that opportunity, I may not come back in the fall." They do not need to make that choice. The more a Christian chooses, the more opportunities he has to fall into making bad choices. Temptation is found in multiple choices.

Jesus fought the Tempter by removing the power to choose. How did Jesus handle the Tempter? When Satan confronted Him with multiple choices, Jesus said, "I don't know what I think about that, but it is written. God has decided for Me." When Satan tempted Jesus to turn the stones into bread, Jesus said, "God chose for Me not to do that. God chose what He wants Me to have—the Word of God."

Satan said, "Jesus, why don't You jump off the pinnacle of the temple?"

Jesus said, "If I chose to do that, I may or may not make the right choice, so I will let God choose for Me; and it is written, 'Thou shalt not tempt the Lord thy God.'"

"If the Son of God knew enough not to choose to answer the Devil, why would Christians make so many choices?"

Satan said, "Why don't You fall down and worship me, and I'll give You all these kingdoms."

Jesus said, "I really don't want to tell you My opinion about that because God made the choice for Me, when He said, 'Thou shalt worship the LORD thy God and him only shalt thou serve.'" Jesus was astute.

If the Son of God knew enough not to choose to answer the Devil, why would Christians make so many choices? If a single guy is out with his girlfriend and he asks her if she wants to have a little "fun," he has no right to put that choice in front of her. I Thessalonians 4:1-7 already tells them both how to behave and

The Source of Temptation

to avoid fornication. God already chose for them. A Christian has no business choosing lover's lane. A Christian young man has no business saying to a young lady, "You don't mind if I put my arm around you, do you?" Yes, she minds because God already said it's wrong to do that in I Corinthians 6:19-20, *"What? know ye not that your body is the temple of the Holy Ghost which is in you, which ye have of God, and ye are not your own? For ye are bought with a price: therefore glorify God in your body, and in your spirit, which are God's."*

A girl says, "What bikini would I look good in?"

God says, "None of them!" It doesn't matter if a girl thinks she looks good or fat or pretty or ugly. Her body is not hers! She should not decide what she wears—God does!

When Christians start making choices about what they want to wear and what they want to drink and where they want to go, they are getting on dangerous ground because they are using the choosing "gun" in a way that God did not intend for them to use it. Multiple choices always get a person into trouble.

When Satan realized he could not get Jesus to exercise His power of choice, he knew he was defeated. The reason Christians get into temptation and fall and struggle and get into sin is that they make choices they have no business choosing.

Let me make several statements about choices.

> *"The reason Christians get into temptation and fall and struggle and get into sin is that they make choices they have no business choosing."*

1. Don't choose when you are confused. Those who say, "I wonder if I should stay or leave" should not choose. God doesn't wear a wristwatch. God doesn't even use the same calendar that we use. Just because college graduation is in May means nothing to God. Teachers will sometimes say, "It's the end of May; I wonder if I ought to leave." What if the same logic was applied to every other area of life: "It's May—I wonder if I should stay married." "It's the end of the school year—should I get rid of my kids?" "It's April—I better quit my job at Ford Motor Company." Decisions should not be reevaluated primarily because a specific time of the year has arrived.

2. **Don't choose when you are hurt.** When a person's heart is about to break, that is the wrong time to decide what he should do about anything. He shouldn't choose anything about his life or about college or about marriage or about money without asking for advice from someone who is a neutral arbitrator.

> *"Decisions should not be reevaluated primarily because a specific time of the year has arrived."*

3. **Don't choose when you are tempted.** Jesus didn't. When a person is facing temptation, he should not say, "I have to do something about this." No, he doesn't. The choice has been made. Just do right.

4. **Don't choose when you are weak.** A person should not choose when he is tired and worn out. One should not choose when he is having a tough time with relationships. When a husband and wife are fussing, that is no time to decide what they think about marriage.

As the pastor of a large church, I am faced with over a thousand decisions a week in my office. But I do not make but two or three of those decisions. Most decisions are already made for me by the Bible, by First Baptist Church policies established over time, and by principles.

In counseling, the counselor usually takes less than five seconds of listening to the person to decide what he is going to tell him. A marriage counselor should set down in writing a list of procedures he will tell people. He should not make up advice as he goes. Principles should already be laid down so the counselor knows what he is supposed to say. A prudent counselor's choices should be defined by policy and principles based on the Word of God. A counselor should rarely make any choices. A good rule of thumb for giving counsel might be, "It is written. It is written. It is written." A counselor should live his whole life that way.

5. Don't choose when no choice needs to be made. College graduates come to my office by the droves and say, "I have five employment opportunities, and all of them tell me I have to let them know my decision by tomorrow."

> *"A prudent counselor's choices should be defined by policy and principles based on the Word of God."*

No one should ever be pressured into making a choice. What do I tell a person who is offered a position that requires an immediate answer? I advise him to say, "I don't know yet." If they turn you down, realize that they were calling when you weren't looking, and there will be more looking for you long after the others are gone.

If anyone says, "You have to decide right now," back up and say, "No, I don't." Never let anybody pressure you to make a choice.

One day somebody was banging on my office door. A piece of paper was eventually slid under the door, and the person kept banging on my door. Finally, I opened the door and the person said, "Pastor, I have to see you *right now*! I have a big decision I have to make *right now*!"

I said, "I don't. Come back Sunday and see me."

"You don't understand," he said. "I have to decide *right now*!"

I said, "Anything that you have to decide right now is a bad way to make a decision." That is a standard principle by which decisions should be considered. A wise man once said, "If it's an emergency today, it'll be an emergency tomorrow." If a Christian will stop making choices when no choice has to be made, it takes the pressure off.

6. **Let wiser people than you make the choice for you.** It is usually apparent if a person knows how to use his "choose gun." When a teenager goes to a counselor and says, "Pastor, I'm an 18-year-old high school graduate, what do you think I should do?" first of all, his willingness to seek guidance with his decisions shows a certain level of maturity not found in most teens, or adults for that matter.

When teenagers are asked, "What do you want to do with your life?" some will say, "Well, I've always wanted to...." It really does not matter what he wants to do. What matters is what God wants him to do. Teens will often change their minds about what they desire to do with their life. Sometimes their desires depend on what television program they were watching. If they want to be a doctor, they've probably been watching a medical drama! Their fickle decision-maker fluctuates up and down.

Every little boy wants to grow up to be a fireman or a policeman or a soldier or a NASCAR race car driver or an astronaut. But most boys grow up to do something not even close to what they "always wanted to be." Everyone has dreamed of doing many things. When I was a boy, I dreamed of being a motorcycle evangelist. I wanted to be a stunt pilot and write "Jesus Saves!" in the air. I wanted to go into business with my dad and be a multi-millionaire and finance the Lord's work. Look where God put me. Now, I'm a Baptist preacher! God has a sense of humor.

Wise young people will take their "choice gun" and say, "Dad or Pastor, I am laying down my decision-maker, and I want **you** to make the decision for me." That is about the best choice a young person could ever make. By the way, giving veto power to another regarding decisions is a good choice for anyone.

Jesus had all power given to Him. He could have sent Satan to Hell any time. The Devil was tempting Jesus to use His power to choose. Jesus laid aside His power and said, "It's already been

The Source of Temptation

chosen for Me." All sin involves choosing. If a Christian would stop choosing, he would stop sinning.

Ladies who make menus do not have to choose what to purchase when they go shopping. Their choices are already made for them by the specific ingredients on the menu. However, many ladies go to the grocery store and decide what items to purchase as they are shopping, and they usually walk out with more groceries than they planned to buy.

> *"All sin involves choosing. If a Christian would stop choosing, he would stop sinning."*

The wise Christian will establish a choosing committee to help him with choices. He should have a finance chooser. People who are in financial trouble often go to counselors hoping that they will give them money to bail them out. The counselors should not give them money. The counselor should tell them to stop choosing and to allow the counselor to start choosing for them. Some couples need to turn their checkbooks and credit cards over to someone else and let that person put them on a budget.

A man might say, "I don't make enough money. I'm going to go broke." The simple truth is he makes plenty of money. No doubt, he is making the wrong financial choices.

Every couple should have a marriage chooser. If a couple has a bad marriage, it should occur to them that maybe they don't know how to make good choices in marriage. If they have to go to the counselor's office and say, "Our marriage stinks," the counselor will say, "Okay, do this." Then the wife says, "That ain't gonna work" as if she really knows how to have a happy marriage! She has the divorce attorney's number sticking out of her pocketbook, and yet she knows what will work and what won't work in marriage. How silly for someone who needs wise, prudent counsel to reject that which he or she so desperately needs.

Is God Enough for You?

One day I was witnessing to someone, and I said, "Do you know for sure that you're going to Heaven?"

He said, "No, I don't."

"I do," I responded.

He said, "Wow. Congratulations!"

"I'm saved," I said to him.

He asked, "What does that mean?" After I told the man how to get saved, He said, "Just like that, you can get saved?"

"Yes, just like that! Would you like to get saved?" I asked.

"No. I have my own ways."

I said, "Excuse me, when I asked you if you were sure you were going to Heaven, you said, 'No.' "

He said, "Well, you've got me there."

"How is your way doing?" I asked him.

He answered, "Man, you're confusing me. It's starting to make sense."

"If you told me that you didn't know how to go to Heaven, and your way was the way of uncertainty and my way was salvation," I clarified, "who should make the choice for you?"

He said, "I don't know. What do you think?"

> **"If** Christians would let good, wise choices be made for them by people who have already made good, wise choices, they wouldn't have to make so many choices."

I wish I had that conversation on video. If I know how to get to Heaven and you don't, let me make the choice for you. I want you to go to Heaven.

Every parent should have a "chooser" in their parenting. Find someone who has reared good kids and find out what they did. Stop making choices that will get you into deeper trouble.

7. Let God decide what you believe. Stop telling God what you believe. If a person would say to God, "God, I'm going

The Source of Temptation

to decide right now that whatever You believe, that's what I believe about it," he would be a happier, more secure person. God should have the opportunity to tell us what we believe about everything in His Book.

If Christians would let good, wise choices be made for them by people who have already made good, wise choices, they wouldn't have to make so many choices. Satan is so shrewd to offer us multiple choices. Then, he labors diligently to convince us that we have within ourselves the ability to make the best decisions. How wise we would be to consistently make our decisions based upon the Word of God and principles. God has never made a bad decision. He has a proven record that is worthy of our trust.

CHAPTER FIVE

The Path of Temptation

"For so it was that the children of Israel had sinned against the LORD their God, which had brought them up out of the land of Egypt, from under the hand of Pharaoh king of Egypt, and had feared other gods, And walked in the statutes of the heathen, whom the LORD cast out from before the children of Israel, and of the kings of Israel, which they had made. And the children of Israel did secretly those things that were not right against the LORD their God, and they built them high places in all their cities, from the tower of the watchmen to the fenced city. And they set them up images and groves in every high hill, and under every green tree: And there they burnt incense in all the high places, as did the heathen whom the LORD carried away before them; and wrought wicked things to provoke the LORD to anger: For they served idols, whereof the LORD had said unto them, Ye shall not do this thing. Yet the LORD testified against Israel, and against Judah, by all the prophets, and by all the seers, saying, Turn ye from your evil ways, and keep my commandments and my statutes, according to all the law which I commanded your fathers, and which I sent to you by my servants the prophets. Notwithstanding they would not hear, but hardened their necks, like to the neck of their fathers, that did not believe in the LORD their God. And they rejected his statutes, and his

> "The more mature and spiritual a Christian becomes, the more dangerous is the private world."

66 ❧ Is God Enough for You?

covenant that he made with their fathers, and his testimonies which he testified against them; and they followed vanity, and became vain, and went after the heathen that were round about them, concerning whom the LORD had charged them, that they should not do like them. And they left all the commandments of the LORD their God, and made them molten images, even two calves, and made a grove, and worshipped all the host of heaven, and served Baal. And they caused their sons and their daughters to pass through the fire, and used divination and enchantments, and sold themselves to do evil in the sight of the LORD, to provoke him to anger." (II Kings 17:7-17)

The Word of God is filled with passages similar to these verses in II Kings which give a quick survey of what Israel had done in the past and the choices they had made which led them into trouble. They made other choices which got them deeper and deeper into trouble. Likewise, Christians get themselves into trouble when they get reckless with their "choice gun" and make choices and decisions on their own. Sometimes the results can be devastating.

A pastor has a tremendous struggle. He must strongly warn those who are going astray in strong, firm, definitive language that says, "You don't want to go that way"; while at the same time, the pastor must say to those who have gone the wrong way, "There is mercy and compassion and a second chance with God." If a pastor is too soft by saying, "There's always a second chance," then the pastor takes the risk of the adults and young people saying, "What's the use. I don't need to stay right. If I do get in trouble, the pastor and the staff will be there to help me; and the Lord is always merciful. So, who cares how I act?"

There are certain things a Christian trades off the further down the slide he goes. Yes, the pastor and Christian brothers will always be there with outstretched arms like the prodigal son's

The Path of Temptation

daddy was. No matter how many harlots on which the son wasted his money and no matter what kind of debauchery in which he participated, the father received him back and put a ring on his finger and threw a party for him. However, that is a small benefit to receive for what he lost. As the elder son found out, dad threw one party for the prodigal son, but the son who stayed home had the entire estate. The prodigal son enjoyed a little bit of fun, but he lost many benefits.

A church member can never sin to the point that he should not be welcome in church. The Christian cannot sin so far that God is not willing to extend mercy and help to him. However, with every step the Christian takes into sin, he forfeits another level of opportunity and joy and gladness. The pastor can get the backslider happy again, but there are things the pastor cannot restore to him. The pastor cannot take away the nagging in the Christian's mind and heart that says, "What if I had not done that?"

> "With every step the Christian takes into sin, he forfeits another level of opportunity and joy and gladness."

If a Christian falls, there are still wonderful opportunities for him, and he can still be extremely productive for God. But, he also forfeits many opportunities that can never be returned to him. The pastor has to preach strong enough to let the Christian know that if he goes down the road of temptation, he won't like himself when he gets there. It is not so much God pointing His long finger in the Christian's face; it is the backslidden Christian pointing his own finger in his own face. Most people do not do all they could do because they get so preoccupied with the mistakes they have made.

II Kings 17:9 says, *"And the children of Israel did secretly those things that were not right against the LORD their God...."* The Christian lives in many worlds. He lives in the world of church where he wears his "Sunday-go-to-meeting" clothes. He listens to church music, he has a songbook in his hands, and he has a Bible in his lap.

The Christian also lives in the world of his home. It's a world in which he spends considerable amounts of time. Many Christians never bring the world of church into the world of home. Some of our bus kids live in a place where the world of home is light years away from the world of church. The world of home competes with the world of church.

On Monday morning, the Christian enters the world of work or the world of school. He may have a different set of friends at work or school than his friends in the world of church. Then, there is the world of socializing. Maybe this world is bowling league buddies, baseball or softball teammates, video game friends, movies friends, or golfing buddies. Then many have the world of hobbies. Some common hobbies might be hunting, fishing, biking, walking, shopping, or any number of other various preferences that occupy time.

Then there is another world that everyone has—his private world. That private world is not the church world or the home world or the work world or the school world or the social world or the hobby world. It is a world in which there is no one but you. It is the individual with all his thoughts and emotions and secrets by himself. Mom and Dad are not welcome in this world. Spouses are not welcome in this world. Not even friends are welcome in this world—a world in which many Christians would prefer not to include God.

"The more mature and spiritual a Christian becomes, the more dangerous is the private world."

The more mature and spiritual a Christian becomes, the more dangerous is the private world. This is a world where very good people get into very big trouble. It is a world that most reveals

The Path of Temptation   69

what a person really is. In the other worlds of an individual, the group embodies a certain personality in each world. In the social world, most people pretty much blend in with the people with whom they associate. The same is true of the work world, the school world, and the church world. With these thoughts in mind, consider the five steps on the path of temptation.

1. The Christian has different worlds in his life and is a different person in each world. In the life of a Christian, each world is segregated uniquely from every other world—each world is totally cut off from the other worlds. In other words, the world of church is a secret world that the friends in another world don't know much about. Then, the home world is a secret world that is kept private. So, as a rule, the Christian totally separates each world from the others, so much so that some wives have no idea what their husbands do at work. The husband keeps his work world separate from his home world.

When the Christian segregates his worlds and he is one person in one world and a different person in each of his other worlds, it is very easy to step into the secret world and be another totally different person than he is in any other world. That is where many Christians stumble terribly.

When the neighbors of a mass murderer are interviewed, they often say, "He was the nicest neighbor." Some said that serial killer Jeffrey Dahmer was as polite a young man as you would ever want to meet. These types of people are a different type of person in each of their worlds. When a Christian cannot find constancy in his life and he has to cut off each world from the others, then he opens the door to have a secret world where he is radically different from what people outwardly know about him.

We should desire to live our lives in such a way that if someone sees us at home or church or in the mall or anywhere else, that we pretty much are the same kind of person. There are certain roles we must play in each world, but we should want to be the same basic person in each world. If we do not find a constancy of person in each of our worlds, we will open the door to being a radically different person in our secret private world.

> "*If we do not find a constancy of person in each of our worlds, we will open the door to being a radically different person in our secret world.*"

Every individual has a private world. A husband has a world in which his wife is not a part. We all have a world where we know our sins and weaknesses. We have a world where no one else is welcome. However, if someone would see us in that world, that person should discover that we are about the same person as in all our other worlds. The nation of Israel developed a different secret life in each of their worlds. They did not have a constancy in their worlds.

I was invited to a meeting at the White House where I met a pastor friend who was also invited. My pastor friend said, "I have no idea why I'm here. I **know** why you're here. You are the pastor of the largest church in America."

I told him, "Don't sell yourself short." My pastor friend was the same at the White House as at any other time I have seen him. He's always promoting and exalting someone else and deprecating himself. He was the same friend for whom I have preached many times. As we chatted with each other, we picked up right where we left off. It was just like he and I saw each other on a regular basis. The beauty of that characteristic shows his members that they have a constancy in their pastor. I want my members to know that they have a constancy in their pastor.

Some of the students that attend a Christian school have a school world look. They also have a social-crowd world look. They follow dress standards when they are at school, and they may wear the proper sports uniform, but they are radically differ-

The Path of Temptation

ent in their private world. I may not be able to make all my worlds blend, but I can be the same guy in all of them. That is the crux of why some stumble in the Christian life.

Often teenagers will speak of their home world and say, "You should hear Dad and Mom on the way to church! You should hear them barking at each other and bickering with each other and yelling and screaming at each other. Then, they get out of the car and go into the church and sweetly say, 'Hello, brother. How are you doing? God sure is good.'"

The children may look confusingly at those actions and say, "What dad is that? You are in my father's body, but who are you?!" Sometimes there are witnesses to how we behave in specific worlds in which we live.

A student was supposed to come see me one day because he was in trouble. His teacher told me, "I don't think he wants to come see you."

"Tell him he **must** come see me," I declared.

"Pastor, he is terrified to walk in your office and see you," the teacher insisted. "The young man told me 'If the Preacher is going to treat me like he preaches in the pulpit, he is going to eat my lunch and ream me out.'"

I said, "Does the boy ever laugh when I preach?"

"I'm sure he does."

I said, "Ask the boy what kind of a guy I am as a man in the pulpit."

The teacher went back and asked the student, "What kind of guy is the Preacher in the pulpit?"

He said, "Well, if he'll be the kind of guy he is in the pulpit, then I can meet that guy in his office."

I am the same man in my office. I don't walk into my office with some pompous attitude. I'm the same preacher in the office as I am in the pulpit. I'm the same guy. Now, in the pulpit I do

Is God Enough for You?

yell, and I hit my fist, and I kick the pulpit. I'm commanded by God to *"Cry aloud, spare not."* (Isaiah 58:1a) That's not my personality, but I'm supposed to do it. However, the me that is the real me is the same me in the pulpit, in my office, in my home, in all the other worlds, and it better be the same me in my private world.

The men who work for me have to be the same in all their different worlds. I don't want them to be one person on Sunday and a different person on Monday and a different person in their homes. No! They ought to have the same kinds of marriages about which I preach. They had better have the same home world as their church world.

A pastor called me recently, and he said, "My kids think I have two different worlds. How do I tell them that I'm busy building a church? How do my kids understand that?"

I said, "It's not the job of the kids to understand that you're a church builder. It's the job of your kids to know that they have a daddy. You'd better be a daddy in the pulpit also. You'd better get up and tell your people that you are not going to choose between serving God and having a happy home." Pastors should never fall for the lie of the Devil that they have to either serve God or build a happy home! No! Have both! I want a happy marriage, **and** I want to be a successful pastor. I want to be a successful soul winner, **and** I want to be a righteous Christian and a decent citizen. I want to be able to shake the hand of the President and then kneel and talk to God and not be a hypocrite in either case.

> *"I want to be able to shake the hand of the President and then kneel and talk to God and not be a hypocrite in either case."*

The Christian must decide. Does he want the church man at home? Many wives would love to have a church man at home. It

The Path of Temptation

would be nice to have some of the home men at church. Some men are dedicated to their families. They never miss family time. They love their wives and children. However, they never win a soul to Christ. They never walk down the aisle and pray at the altar. They never move with any kind of affection or passion in church, but they have the most wonderful home in the whole world. But their church life stinks!

A teenage boy once said to me, "My dad has to be one of the best human men God put on this earth."

I said, "I'm happy for you."

He said, "I'm not. He never goes to church. He never reads his Bible. He never prays. I don't even know if he's saved or not." Men need to be the same in all their different worlds.

A man may be a phenomenal worker at his place of employment. However, he never brings his church world into his work world. He may curse at work, but he is an excellent worker. If someone went to the boss and said, "Do you know so-and-so?" he'd say, "You know so-and-so? He's one of the best workers I have, but he cusses a blue streak." Which man is he? In that situation, what is scary is that man also has a private world. If the difference in his church world and his work world are an indication of what he is, then it might be terrifying to know about that man's private world where nobody knows what he is really like.

When a Christian goes to work, the people at work ought to know that he is a born-again, independent, fundamental Baptist who loves Jesus Christ. That doesn't mean that a man is supposed to preach at work. No, he is supposed to be working. However, everyone ought to know that he loves the Lord, that he doesn't curse or

> "When a Christian goes to work, the people at work should know that he is a born-again, independent, fundamental Baptist who loves Jesus Christ."

smoke or drink or tell the filthy jokes or laugh at others' filthy jokes. Christian men have no business going in the break rooms at work where the men have hung indecent pictures of women. A Christian should work hard and be a good testimony where the people with whom he works will say, "That Christian over there sure is a hard worker."

Landlords should know that their Christian renters pay their rent on time or early, never cheat their landlord, never ask for an extension of time, and they leave their apartments or houses clean and tidy when they move out. That is a world that is seen by only a few, but the actions speak volumes.

Some men have a wonderful home world, but they never let their work world know about it. A man should be known at work as a man who loves one woman—his wife. When a fellow worker says, "Hey, did you see that woman?" the man ought to say, "She's not as pretty as my wife."

"When a Christian is different in each of his worlds, he opens the door to being extremely perverted in his private world."

When a Christian is different in each of his worlds, he opens the door to being extremely perverted in his private world. This is when the wife comes to the counselor's office and says, "You won't believe what my husband is into. He is having an affair and is leaving me."

2. Not only should the Christian be a consistent person in each world, but God should be invited to enter each world. The Christian must invite God into each of his worlds. The church should include God in every aspect. God should be in every classroom, on every bus route, in every nursery, and in every song. God should be allowed to have preeminence in every part and every world of the Christian. The Lord of Glory should have preeminence and be magnified in every home. The Christian should be the same person at home, but he should also

The Path of Temptation

have the same Person in his home also—the Lord Jesus Christ.

When the Christian goes to work, he should be the same person, but he should also have the same person with him—the Lord Jesus Christ. Jesus should be in every world in the Christian's life. Jesus Christ should get the glory from our little league baseball teams. God should be the center of every world. The problem with some Christian teenagers is that they have a friend world where Jesus is not welcome, and that is why they bring shame and reproach to their parents and shame to the testimony of Jesus Christ.

The Israelites had secret worlds out of which they left God. If God is to be in all the different worlds, then He must be in a person's private world. The happy person is the one who does not seek to have a secret world where just he exists. That is when men get their dirty magazines. That is when people have their affairs. That is when wicked music is allowed into the outward life of the Christian.

If a Christian will leave God out of his work world, he will dead sure leave God out of His private world. If a Christian will leave God out of his family, he will leave God out of his private world. If a Christian refuses to include God in his church world, he will also shove God from his private world.

Charles G. Finney lived in the late 1700's and early 1800's. He was the president of Oberlin College in Ohio. One day he was invited by a friend to go to the Masonic lodge. He agreed to go. The head man in the lodge recognized Mr. Finney as a very famous preacher. At the end of their meeting, the head man said, "We have a very famous preacher with us today, Charles Finney. Mr. Finney, would you come and dismiss our meeting in prayer." Mr. Finney left his seat, walked to the front, and stood before the men.

He said, "Let's bow for prayer." Mr. Finney prayed and closed his prayer with the words, "In Jesus' name we ask. Amen."

The head man met him afterward and said, "Mr. Finney, I'm glad you came to our meeting. However, we have Jewish brethren here and others of non-Christian faiths. It offends them highly if you pray, 'In Jesus' name.' "

Mr. Finney said, "If Jesus Christ is not welcome here, neither is Charles Finney."

Christian, if you can't take Jesus Christ some place, you had better not go there. For example, a Christian should be very uncomfortable in a state university where Jesus Christ is not welcome.

In my high school, there were many born-again Christians. In science class, we looked at the primate chart of evolution. I looked at my friends and said, "Isn't that a bunch of hogwash."

One of them said, "That's science."

I said, "**You** may have come from a monkey, but I didn't. I came from my mama who came from her mama who came from her mama all the way back to Adam and Eve who came from God."

He said, "I believe that too! When the teacher comes in, what are you going to do about it?"

I said, "You are going to stand up and tell him that he's full of baloney."

My friend was one of those kids that was very vocal and outgoing. He said, "I'm going to do that." I knew if I got him interested, he would do it. I was the brains, and he was the mouth! We were all sitting in class when the teacher walked in. He began teaching and said, "We're talking about evolution today. Do you have any questions?"

My outspoken friend stood up and said, "Yes. The majority of us believe that chart is ungodly, un-American, and inappropriate."

The Path of Temptation

I was sitting there thinking, "This is good! This is better than I thought it was going to be."

The teacher looked at the chart and said, "You know what. I agree. That's stupid. Let's pull down the chart. I'm a Christian. I see many of you in church. We all know God made us." The teacher then went on to another lesson! That happened in a public school!

If a Christian cannot bring Jesus Christ into an environment where Jesus is welcome, then he should leave that environment. Many people have to work in environments with non-Christians, but the Christian does not have to socialize with those people. He can take his Bible to work and read it on breaks.

If Jesus Christ is not welcome, then we should not want to be in that particular world. If Jesus is allowed to be unwelcome in one world, then He will be pushed out of our private world. We ought to live a life that tries to make our private world our best world. If our private world is our best world, the rest will all fall into place. We should not desire to be our best at church. We should desire to be our best in secret.

The day I became pastor of the First Baptist Church of Hammond, God pointed out Matthew 6:6 to me. "*But thou, when thou prayest, enter into thy closet, and when thou hast shut thy door, pray to thy Father which is in secret; and thy Father which seeth in secret shall reward thee openly.*" Every time I pray, I open my Bible to Matthew 6:6. I lean my Bible against the wall of my office, and I lie down on the floor facing that verse. I read that verse. I put my hands on that verse in my Bible. Sometimes I bring it to my lips and kiss it. I say, "God, this is the verse I am claiming right here." I want the Father to look at my secret world and say, "If his secret world is that good, I can bless him in all his other worlds."

Some people ask, "Pastor, how do I get God to bless me in my marriage?" My first thought is, "What is that person's private world like?" The issue is not if the husband will change or the wife will change. The Bible says, *"And thy Father which seeth in secret shall reward thee openly."* God will bless the man who makes the secret world the most important world.

3. **When God is not included in the various worlds of the Christian, the Christian will do as the heathen.** II Kings 17:11 says, *"And there they burnt incense in all the high places, as did the heathen…."* When the Christian cannot bring Christ into his different worlds, then he will conform and blend with the people in those worlds.

Many Christians have chosen to copy one of two avenues because the heathen make it so easy to copy them. The Christian turns on the television and copies the people on the television. He turns on the music video and copies that. He turns on the rock 'n' roll CD and copies that. The clothing that some teenagers wear comes straight from the music industry. The music industry sets the styles; Hollywood is the mouthpiece for the styles. Music rules the world. The Christian falls prey and copies the heathen.

The Christian will copy somebody—he will copy either the Lord Jesus Christ and the pattern given in the Word of God, or he will copy the world in which he is living. If a child goes to a public school, he will either copy the Bible or the kids in the school. If a child goes to a Christian school, he will copy either the good crowd or the bad crowd. Perhaps a person curses because he copies the cursing heathen. A person may say, "I have a problem with cursing." It is probably because he is listening to cursing at work or on the television or in his music. My Bible says, *"Let no corrupt communication proceed out of your mouth,"* (Ephesians 4:29a) *"Let your speech be alway with grace, seasoned with salt."* (Colossians 4:6a) The Bible says our communication should be helpful, medicinal, and flavorful; and not vulgar, distasteful, or unholy. But the reason we have vulgar language is that we are copying the heathen.

The videos many Christians watch are full of cursing. After church, Christians rush home and watch a filthy video or the fools on television with all the filthy talk and sexual innuendoes and the perverted thinking of fools. When the Christian does that, he will copy the heathen in his life. Even a casual observer of the life of Jesus Christ would admit that Jesus would not have viewed the fools and heathen that are prominently displayed on television shows and in the music industry.

Outside the judgment hall trial of Jesus when Peter wanted to prove to the "world" with which he was running—a world of Christ deniers—that he was **not** one of Christ's followers, he first denied knowing Jesus, and then he cursed. Christians cannot watch or listen to the profanity of the world and say, "I don't have any problem with my private world."

The Christian is going to have to decide sometime in his life how much of Jesus he wants in the world in which he lives. "More about Jesus would I learn. More of His holy will discern." The next time you're about to go to your favorite video store, put on your favorite song that reminds you how good God is to you. Then go to your private world and say, "Does that song describe my private world?" Then walk into your video store and say, "I want to rent all the Christ-honoring, God-fearing, righteous, and holy videos." The clerk would say, "Both of those are checked out."

4. When God is not included in the worlds of a Christian, wise prudent warnings go unheeded. Once a Christian is a different person in each of his worlds and he has a private world where even Jesus Christ is not welcome, then he starts copying the heathen people in his worlds; then when the preacher gets up and says, "You had better get more of God into your worlds," he shuts off the preacher.

I marvel at the ability of some Christians to shut off the preacher! People should wake up and listen to the man of God! I am flabbergasted how some people come to my office and ask me the most foolish questions, and I say, "Do you ever listen to me preach?" One person said, "I don't. I have shut you off since the day you became pastor." And those folks wonder why they have problems!

II Kings 17:13, 14 says, *"Yet the* LORD *testified against Israel, and against Judah, by all the prophets, and by all the seers, saying, Turn ye from your evil ways, and keep my commandments and my statutes, according to all the law which I commanded your fathers, and which I sent to you by my servants the prophets. Notwithstanding they would not hear, but hardened their necks, like to the neck of their fathers, that did not believe in the* LORD *their God."* It would have been much easier if Israel had listened to the prophets. God sent them Isaiah, Jeremiah, Ezekiel, Daniel, Amos, Obadiah, Elijah, Elisha and so many others. The wise, prudent warnings God sent by His prophets to Israel went unheeded.

5. When God is not included in the worlds of a Christian, the Christian will go after the heathen and make them his heroes. II Kings 17:15-16, *"And they rejected his statutes, and his covenant that he made with their fathers, and his testimonies which he testified against them; and they followed vanity, and became vain, and went after the heathen that were round about them, concerning whom the* LORD *had charged them, that they should not do like them. And they left all the commandments of the* LORD *their God, and made them molten images, even two calves, and made a grove, and worshipped all the host of heaven, and served Baal."* First, Israel did as the heathen did. These verses state that they went after the heathen.

If some ladies were asked to give up their soap operas, they

The Path of Temptation

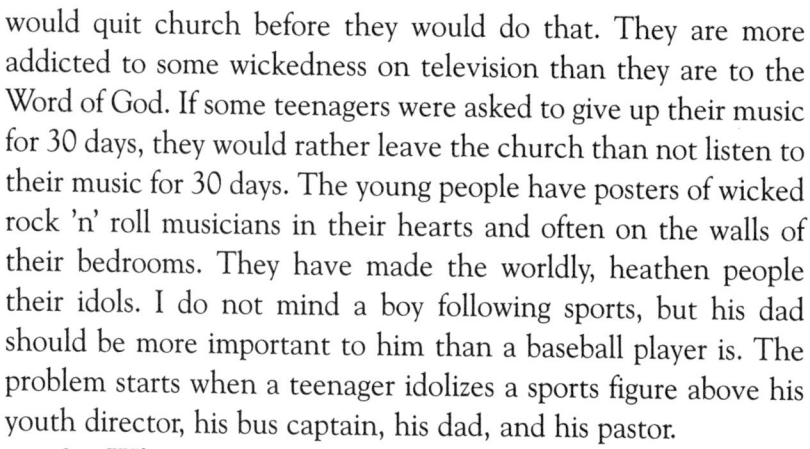

would quit church before they would do that. They are more addicted to some wickedness on television than they are to the Word of God. If some teenagers were asked to give up their music for 30 days, they would rather leave the church than not listen to their music for 30 days. The young people have posters of wicked rock 'n' roll musicians in their hearts and often on the walls of their bedrooms. They have made the worldly, heathen people their idols. I do not mind a boy following sports, but his dad should be more important to him than a baseball player is. The problem starts when a teenager idolizes a sports figure above his youth director, his bus captain, his dad, and his pastor.

  6. **When God is not included in the worlds of a Christian, someone will eventually suffer the consequences.** II Kings 17:17, *"And they caused their sons and their daughters to pass through the fire, and used divination and enchantments, and sold themselves to do evil in the sight of the LORD, to provoke him to anger."* Most Bible teachers would teach that these people were offering their children to idols, particularly Molech. Molech was the god of whoremongers. His figure was a seated statue with a fire burning in his lap, picturing the hot passions of immorality. His hands would be curled upward above his lap. The people would place their babies in the hands of Molech. The baby was the fruit of illegitimacy. The baby would be offered to appease Molech, the god of whoremongers, and then the person would go out and commit fornication again.

  The phrase *"through the fire"* means that they forced their children, by their private perversions, to suffer for their wicked worlds. If a person bore all the punishment of his wickedness, that would be one thing. However, that is not how it works. God said that He visits a person's iniquity to the first, second, third, and fourth generations. For four generations, the consequences of a person's sins will have to be dealt with by his descendants. He is forcing his family to go **"through the fire."**

Is God Enough for You?

I do not understand how women can destroy the life of an unborn baby and say, "It is our body and our life." Who will be a voice for the yet unborn child, because he has no voice? Where are the groups who are devoted to standing up for the little guy? How little do you have to be to have a voice? Hey, Mr. leader of an advocate group—well-heeled, spoiled-rotten, heathen hypocrites—why aren't those groups doing what they were founded for—groups who were to be a voice for the oppressed people who don't have a voice? I can give them a million and a half people who are killed every year who had no voice! All those supposed one million women who marched on Washington because they wanted their right to make a choice—who gets to choose for their unborn children? Those in favor of abortion are in favor of murdering.

I don't understand how parents can flippantly break up their homes. Christian couples who shake their fists at God and say out of one side of their mouth, "We are going to dissolve our marriage," are saying out of the other side of their mouth to their children, "And **you** are going to pay the price!" The children who have to grow up in divorced homes come to my office by the droves with emotional scars on them and say, "Please tell married couples to stay together." Couples who seek divorce are no different than those heathen that want to murder their babies and no different from those who want to rape and pillage and violate and steal and cheat and lie and corrupt. By their very actions they are saying, "I have my right to live my life, and I'll live in my world the way I want to live." Yes, and those couples are making their children pass through the fire. The children are forced to feel the singed hair of the hot passion of their parents because their parents couldn't say "No." Those children have a right to a voice also. Those parents are violating their children and making them go through the fire because of their parents' fornication and sexual immorality. Those parents are taking away the voice of their children and saying, "You have no voice about how I live in my private world."

How vital it is for Christians to include the Lord God in every world of their lives, especially in their private, secret world. The stakes are high. Satan desires nothing more than for a Christian to think of himself as an island unto himself. But the simple truth is that when the Christian succumbs to the temptation of making his own decisions in his own way, someone will eventually feel the pain of those careless decisions.

CHAPTER SIX

The Great Distraction

"And as Jesus passed by, he saw a man which was blind from his birth. And his disciples asked him, saying, Master, who did sin, this man, or his parents, that he was born blind? Jesus answered, Neither hath this man sinned, nor his parents: but that the works of God should be made manifest in him. I must work the works of him that sent me, while it is day: the night cometh, when no man can work. As long as I am in the world, I am the light of the world." (John 9:1-5)

John chapter nine is a chapter of debate. Here is a man who has been blind from birth. The disciples of Jesus met him and got into a quizzical debate wondering why this man was blind. Could his parents be guilty of some great sin and God is judging them by giving them a blind child? Did the parents have a defect in their genetics that caused the blindness of their child? The disciples debated among themselves as to the cause of this man's blindness?

"As long as the Christian has to have his life's problems solved, then God is on constant trial as to whether or not He is good."

The debate continued in verses 8 and 9 when the neighbors got involved. *"The neighbours therefore, and they which before had seen him that he was blind, said, Is not this he that sat and begged?*

86 ❧ Is God Enough for You?

Some said, This is he: others said, He is like him: but he said, I am he."

Then the debate changed to how this blind man's eyes were opened. Verse 10 continues, *"Therefore said they unto him, How were thine eyes opened?"*

In verse 16, another issue was brought into the picture. *"Therefore said some of the Pharisees, This man is not of God, because he keepeth not the sabbath day. Others said, How can a man that is a sinner do such miracles? And there was a division among them."* The religious crowd became involved in the debate saying, "Was Jesus worthy to perform this miracle?"

One said, "Of course He is not worthy!"

Another said, "If He's not worthy, then the miracle couldn't have taken place."

Yet another declared, "Well, the blind man can now see!"

The whole chapter unfolds with the disciples debating, the neighbors getting involved, and the religious crowd arguing over the miracle. Jesus was listening on the sidelines. He said almost nothing in the entire chapter. He was just listening to the argument.

Then in verses 18-21, the Jews doubted that the man was even blind. *"But the Jews did not believe concerning him, that he had been blind, and received his sight, until they called the parents of him that had received his sight. And they asked them, saying, Is this your son, who ye say was born blind? how then doth he now see? His parents answered them and said, We know that this is our son, and that he was born blind: But by what means he now seeth, we know not; or who hath opened his eyes, we know not: he is of age; ask him: he shall speak for himself."*

The disciples are arguing; the neighbors are involved; the Pharisees are arguing about it; the Jews become involved. All this over one man who had a problem that was solved, and now an entire nation is arguing about the situation.

The Great Distraction

The intensity of the situation continued to increase in verses 24-25, "*Then again called they the man that was blind, and said unto him, Give God the praise: we know that this man is a sinner. He answered and said, Whether he be a sinner or no, I know not: one thing I know, that, whereas I was blind, now I see.*"

The healed man had been listening to everybody hollering and arguing. Then he said, "I know one thing: I was blind a while ago and now I can see. You all can figure out how it happened, Who did it, and if He was worthy or not! But I can see!"

Verses 28-29 say, "*Then they reviled him, and said, Thou art his disciple; but we are Moses' disciples. We know that God spake unto Moses: as for this fellow, we know not from whence he is.*" Then the debate changed to who was the right religious leader to follow.

Jesus is still quietly standing off and listening. He speaks but a few lines during the whole debate. In answer to the question about who had sinned and caused this man to be blind, Jesus had said in verses 3-5, "*Jesus answered, Neither hath this man sinned, nor his parents: but that the works of God should be made manifest in him. I must work the works of him that sent me, while it is day: the night cometh, when no man can work. As long as I am in the world, I am the light of the world.*"

Then he said to the blind man in verse 7, "*...Go, wash in the pool of Siloam....*"

The next time Jesus spoke was in verse 35, "*...Dost thou believe on the Son of God?*" and then in verse 37, "*...Thou hast both seen him, and it is he that talketh with thee.*"

Jesus continues in verse 39, "*...For judgment I am come into this world, that they which see not might see; and that they which see might be made blind.*"

In this debate I find just a sampling of what the average Christian's life is like.

1. **Each Christian has life-size problems.** His problem may

be blindness as was this man's problem in John. It may be blindness or deafness or a damaged marriage or a wayward child or financial problems. It may be a problem with a relative, a problem at work, a problem holding down a job, a problem finding a job, a problem with a neighbor or another person, a problem with the government, or a variety of other life-size problems.

2. God never suggests one time that we can or should live problem free. Jesus never said that He would fix all our problems. So often when I counsel people, they have this idea that they are supposed to be pursuing this Utopia where they get to problem-free living; and then they will get about the business of living life. While they are living their life, they are missing the opportunities afforded them. They are so wrapped up in their life-size problems and trying to get to a problem-free zone that they are forfeiting many opportunities.

Jesus happened to heal the blind man in John chapter 9. However, there were many blind people in the Bible who never got healed. Why doesn't God heal deaf Christians? Why doesn't God heal blind Christians that faithfully attend church?

Every Sunday as I walk down the alley behind our church, I shake hands with about 300 people. In that line of people, there are two little blind girls that meet me every week to give me a penny. They hear my voice as I greet people in the alley, and when I get close to them, the other family members say, "Here comes Pastor now." I put my hand out and get down close to them where they can hear me, and I say, "I see two of the prettiest girls I've ever seen. What do you girls have for me?" They each put a penny into my hand because they have heard me say that when I see a penny, I feel God is saying, "I love you, Jack." I shake their hands and compliment them. They are precious little girls who have never seen their pastor and probably never will this side of eternity. For some reason, God has not healed them.

The Great Distraction

If I were God, I would heal those girls. They are precious little girls who never miss church. But God has not chosen to heal them. Why doesn't God heal them? Why doesn't God heal the problems of Christians? Why doesn't God remove the marriage problems of some Christians? Why doesn't God make all our children turn out right? Why doesn't God fix all our relationship problems? Everybody has life-size problems. It must not be God's will for the Christian to live problem-free because He keeps giving more problems to us.

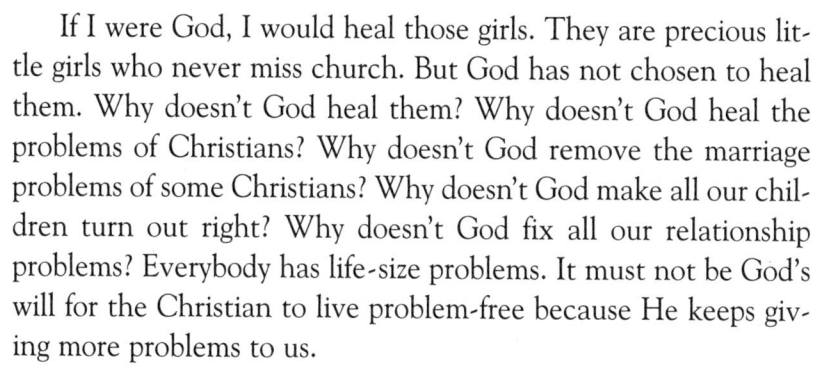

Every time I am about to get rid of a problem, I turn the corner and there's a huge accident in front of me! One problem leads to another problem.

3. **Our sin nature is a constant irritation in our lives and relationships.** The older we get, the more the sin nature will cause problems. The Christian's sin nature will be with him until he gets his brand new body in Heaven.

4. **Worldly issues compete for the Christian's attention.** We are in the world. I hate to go shopping because I have to see the worldly advertisements and the worldly ways that people dress and the downplaying of decency and the uplifting of ungodliness. I have to listen to wicked music. By the time I get home, I want to smash the gift I bought for somebody! The world irritates me. To the fleshly appetites that I have subdued, the world says, "Liven them up!"

Churches change. They bring in the drum sets and the rock music. I get frustrated when Christians get into debates. There are some issues we must debate over; for example, which Bible is the right Bible—the King James Bible is the only one! I get tired of all the fussing and debating and arguing.

People come to my office and say, "We have marital problems." They are married; that's why! I know of no couples who can honestly say they have never had a cross word with each other. They are trying to find an existence that doesn't exist in the mind of God. Christians are looking for a financial utopia, marital utopia—a problem-free life. It doesn't exist!

A man came to me one day and said, "Pastor, I'm ashamed to admit this. I'm 35 years old, and I'm in debt."

I said, "I'm 46 and in debt!"

"You have to be kidding," he said.

We are stuck on this little ball of dirt spinning around. We have life-size problems. We have the flesh nature afflicting us. We have the world trying to distract us. We have Satan trying to tempt us. I'm surprised that any people do right nowadays—and yet, we can!

5. **God has a great work He wants each Christian to do.** In John 9, after all the debating, finally someone asked Jesus what He thought about the situation, and in verse 4 Jesus said, "*I must work the works of him that sent me, while it is day: the night cometh, when no man can work.*" I love that approach. Jesus was telling them, "I did not come here to heal all the blind. I did not come here to heal all the deaf." Jesus' purpose for coming was the same purpose intended for every man—to work the works of Him that sent us.

> "God is not in the business of healing everyone; however, He is in the business of helping Christians focus on a great work He has for us to do."

I was talking to a member of an area church who believes in faith healing. They had recently had a well-known faith healer to preach at their church. This member said, "Why don't you come and hear So-and-So when he comes to our church?"

I said, "Who is So-and-So?"

He said, "Everybody he touches is healed!"

I said, "I thought the famous faith healer did that. Why do you need somebody else?" After Preacher So-and-So leaves, that

The Great Distraction

church will have some other great faith healer come in. That's all tomfoolery! God is not in the business of healing everyone; however, He is in the business of helping Christians focus on a great work He has for us to do.

In verse 3, Jesus says that God has works that He wants to manifest in the lives of Christians. Jesus was saying that as long as He was in the world, He was going to do the work of God. He was to be a light testifying for God. Jesus was also saying that He might heal somebody, but that was not why He came. He came to do great works for God, and He intended to let nothing distract Him from doing those works.

By focusing on the work He was sent to do, Jesus is teaching us several lessons:

A. Life's problems should not paralyze the Christian into doing nothing for God. The problems of life for the Christian should not paralyze the Christian so that all he thinks about and all he endeavors to do is to get away from that problem. Most problems in life will not be solved this side of the grave. Only death will solve many of life's problems.

A marriage may be afflicted for 15 or 20 years. A spouse may say, "I'll just get divorced." That won't fix the problem any more than disowning your children will fix the problems between parents and children. A person can run and hide or change his name and identity, but there is one great problem with that: he takes himself with him. Who that person is and what he has been becoming are what got him into the problem he is facing. If he leaves, everything he has been becoming goes with him. Leaving would be a great solution if a person could change his past, change who he is, and divorce himself from himself. That is impossible.

> "Most problems in life will not be solved this side of the grave. Only death will solve many of life's problems."

92 ❧ Is God Enough for You?

Marriage problems, relationship problems, child-rearing problems, financial problems, employer problems, disappointments, or distress should not keep a Christian from doing the purpose for which God put him on this earth.

A young man said to me, "Pastor, I think the world is coming to an end." Tell me some great prophecy! The world has been coming to an end since Jesus said, "that the last days would come." The world started ending the day God said, *Let there be light.*"

The Christian must not let the problems in the world rattle him. Someone said, "But our nation is at war in Iraq!" Pearl Harbor wasn't exactly a picnic! Christians must live their lives and pursue the purpose of why God put them on earth. Children have been disappointing parents since Adam and Eve had their first son who turned out to be a murderer. Folks, why are we so surprised that the world is filled with life-size problems?

B. The great works of God are not done by those with no problems; the great works of God are done by those who work while working through their problems. When Joseph was in jail and the men came to him asking if he could interpret their dreams, I suppose Joseph could have said, "This is not what I had in mind! Who cares about your stupid dreams!" Two years later Joseph was catapulted out of that dismal situation to the position of second in command because he took time to do a work for God while in prison. If Joseph had been like most Christians, he would have said, "I don't care what you dreamed last night! We're all in jail! Just shut up! I don't care about your problems! I'm a teenage kid who was sold by his brothers! Let me tell you about my problems!"

While the Christian is struggling with his life-size problems, he should get busy doing the works of God. When Dr. and Mrs. Lee Roberson, the former pastor and first lady of the Highland Park Baptist Church in Chattanooga, Tennessee, lost their seven-

The Great Distraction

year-old girl Joy in a tragic accident, that was a life-size problem. Losing a child is a life-size problem. Dr. and Mrs. Roberson said, "Let's start a camp that takes children free of charge." Last time I heard, over 40,000 children were saved at that camp because the Robersons kept on living while working through their life-size problem.

Daniel faced the life-size problem of the lion's den. I suppose the king's decree telling Daniel that if he prayed to anyone except the king he would be executed was a life-size problem. I suppose being ripped out of your homeland and taken captive 500 miles away was a life-size problem. I suppose watching your homeland being burned was a life-size problem. Yet, Daniel did more to open up prophecy than any prophet in the Bible. Daniel, while he was trying to cope with his life-size problem, decided to do the work of God. He wrote the Book of Daniel. He preached. For seven years, he actually ran the Babylonian kingdom while Nebuchadnezzar was coping with his own life-size problems.

If the Christian says in frustration, "Time out, world! I have to deal with my life-size problems!" the world sometimes sarcastically replies, "Sorry. We're like a steamroller. We're going to roll over you, buddy."

A humorous way of looking at how someone might confront his life-size problems is related in the following stories. There's the old golf joke about the man who went golfing with his boss. The man came home three hours late, and his wife was waiting for him at the door. The wife said, "Where have you been?"

He said, "Sweetheart, I was golfing with my boss. On the second hole, my boss teed up his ball, took a back swing, and fell over dead with a heart attack!"

She said, "Oh my goodness. No! What happened?"

Her husband said, "It was brutal the rest of game. Hit the ball, drag the boss. Hit the ball, drag the boss."

94 — Is God Enough for You?

Each one of us has to finish the game of life! Just drag the boss along! Just drag along your life-size problem.

Another man was golfing. He was on the fifteenth hole and ready to tee off. During his back swing, he saw a hearse go by. He laid down his golf club, took off his golf cap, and put it over his heart. His partner said, "What a Southern gentlemen."

As he watched the hearse pass by, the golfer calmly stated, "I was married to her for 12 years."

Whether a Christian is happy or sad, inside or out, he has to go on about his business of serving God. God has given the Christian more to do in life than simply moping and saying, "I can't cope." If life is a challenge, hit the ball of life and drag the problem, but keep on playing the game of life!

A bad marriage shouldn't shut down the whole world. A bad marriage should not stop a person from running his bus route or going on visitation or teaching Sunday school. All life-size problems ought to be confronted by the approach of hitting the ball and dragging those same problems.

C. A Christian must not let the physical blindness keep him from seeing the great opportunities God has for him. Jesus said to the blind man, "You were physically blind, but you knew Who I was. When I spoke to you, you did what I told you to do, and now you are looking at Me." Yet, there were people who could see Jesus who would not hear Him or follow Him. Jesus was saying to the blind man, "Don't get so wrapped up in your need for physical healing; go to work for My Father."

If God chooses to take away a life-size problem, that is not something in which to get so wrapped up that God is forgotten. That a person gets financially turned around and is now financially successful does not give him a right to stop his ministry. Because a couple's bad marriage is now happy doesn't give them the right to say, "We're just going to live on a continual honeymoon" and cause them to quit teaching their Sunday school class. Neither problems nor solutions give the Christian the right to stop playing the game of life.

Jesus said there are a few things a Christian must do while going through his problems.

- **Obey Jesus.** John 9:7 says, "*And said unto him, Go, wash in the pool of Siloam, (which is by interpretation, Sent.) He went his way therefore, and washed, and came seeing.*" Jesus never told that blind man that if he washed in the pool of Siloam he would be healed. Yet, the blind man obeyed Jesus. Likewise, Jesus looks at the Christian and says, "I'm not promising that I am going to fix your problem, but I want you to obey Me."

Single people might be tempted to say, "I'm still single, God. What are You going to do about it?"

God says, "Go join the bus ministry."

The single person asks, "Will I meet my mate there?" God might not necessarily promise anything. He simply tells the single person to obey. Is that the answer to singleness? No. It is the answer to why that person was put on earth—to obey God.

God did not put man on earth to marry. God did not put woman on earth to have babies. God did not put the Christian on earth to make money. God did not put us on earth to be happy. God put mankind on this earth to glorify the Father Who is in Heaven! If blindness or deafness glorifies God, then so be it. If singleness and a barren womb glorify God, then so be it!

One of our members almost lost a child due to an accident. The baby was near death, and the doctors didn't give her much hope. We prayed and prayed. The father called me and said that the baby was going to be okay. We praised God on the phone. A few days later he met me at my office and said, "I'm so happy. Isn't God good!"

I said, "He sure is. But let me tell you something. My grandbaby is in Heaven, and God is good! Your wife gets to hold her child. My daughter doesn't get to hold her baby. But I will tell you something: God is good!"

God is not good because He let one baby live. God is not good because someone is healed. God is not good because some have a nice, shiny automobile. God is not good because some get a pay raise. God is good because God is good! God is not any better because He does good things for us. God is good because He gives us a chance to live on this earth and to glorify the Father which is in Heaven.

God doesn't always come through in a big way like He did for the family of that baby. The opposite situation was true for another couple in our church. I sat in the hospital with them as the father held his dead little baby girl in his arms, and he put a smile on his face and said, "I love God, and God is good, Preacher." Yes, God is good all the time. God is always good.

As long as the Christian has to have his life's problems solved, then God is on constant trial as to whether or not He is good. The Christian is not to decide whether or not God is good, or whether God is worthy of his praise. I am breathing air—God is worthy of my praise! I want my lips to praise Him, and I want my hands to praise Him. I can see—God is good! Others cannot see—God is still good! I can hear, others cannot—God is good! God is *always* good.

> "As long as the Christian has to have his life's problems solved, then God is on constant trial as to whether or not He is good."

God sometimes gives us things to do that we think are tickets to our success. I was talking one day to a pastor who said, "Pastor Schaap, the great church you pastor was built by soul winning, wasn't it?"

I said, "No, it wasn't."

The Great Distraction

"I've been to Pastors' School," he offered. "That church was built by soul winning, wasn't it?"

"No, the First Baptist Church of Hammond was **not** built by soul winning. Jesus said, 'I will build my church.' The First Baptist Church of Hammond was built by Jesus," I explained.

He said, "But Jesus used soul winning to do it. Humanly speaking, soul winning has made the great First Baptist Church."

I said, "Humanly speaking, this church is what it is because of Jesus Christ."

He said, "Do you think soul winning has anything to do with the fact that you have a large church?"

I said, "Yes, God tends to bless obedient Christians more than disobedient Christians. He commanded us to go soul winning, so we go soul winning; and we like to think Jesus has been gracious to want to bless us a little more than those who don't want to go soul winning."

Men who go out and start churches and think soul winning is going to build their church had better fall on their faces and say, "God, I know Who builds a church—You do." Jesus said, "*...upon this rock I will build my church....*" (Matthew 16:18)

We are supposed to go soul winning because we are supposed to obey God. But if God said, "Go into all the world, stand on your head, gargle peanut butter, and quote the twenty-third Psalm backwards in French Portuguese," I would do that! Is soul winning the method to build a church? No. An obedient Christian goes soul winning because God said to do it.

When Jesus told the blind man to go wash in the pool of Siloam, the man did not ask Jesus if he would be healed; he just obeyed Jesus. That man was not healed of his blindness because he washed. He was healed of his blindness because he obeyed. It was not the pool of Siloam that healed the man. It was the power of God exercising His authority where He wanted to, and He happened to want to bless obedience.

A husband may say, "Pastor, if I take my wife out every Friday night for a date, will that improve my marriage?" That is not certain, but the Bible says in Ephesians 5:25, "*Husbands, love your wives, even as Christ also loved the church, and gave himself for it,*" so a husband should take his wife out anyway.

A husband may say, "But my wife is mean and ornery, and she doesn't clean the house." That doesn't matter. The Bible says, "Husbands, love your wives." Will a husband's loving his wife fix their marriage? That is not certain, but we are supposed to obey. It is better to be an obedient Christian so that God can bless us, because God surely does not have a track record for blessing disobedience.

> "*It is better to be an obedient Christian so that God can bless us because God surely does not have a track record for blessing disobedience.*"

The Bible says that wives are to submit themselves to their own husband as unto the Lord. Will that fix their marriage? That is not certain, but God tends to bless obedient wives more than disobedient wives.

- **God wants our faith.** John 9:35 says, "*…Dost thou believe on the Son of God?*" God says that if Christians will obey Him and trust Him, they can do some great works together. While church members are trying to solve their marriage problems, trying to get their children on track, trying to get their finances where they should be, and trying to solve all their life's problems, they are being used of God to build the largest independent fundamental Baptist church in the world. It is not because they are living problem free. It is because they have said, "We're going to hit the ball and drag the boss; hit the ball and drag my problems."

I cannot promise my members who come to me for marriage counseling that I will be able to fix their marriages, but while we are trying to fix their problems, we are trying to build another school in China. While we're trying to solve our life-size problems, we are trying to win the world to Christ! We want to get into all of the over 200 nations! We want to go into China! We want to go into India! We want to go into Bulgaria! We want to go into Albania! We want to go to the whole world and say, "We are not going to let our problems keep us from getting the Gospel to you!" That is the great work of Christianity.

God didn't say, "Go into all the world and repair marriages." God didn't say, "Go into all the world and make all teenagers obey their moms and dads." God didn't say, "Go into all the world and make sure all the brethren get along with each other." God said, "Go into all the world and preach the Gospel to every person."

In Mark 16, the disciples were squabbling with each other. In verse 14, the Bible says that Jesus upbraided the disciples for their unbelief. The word *upbraided* means in our modern day vernacular "rip your face off." Jesus was angry with the disciples. The disciples had been with him for three and a half years, and they still had not figured out that Jesus was the Son of the living God. Jesus upbraided the disciples; then in verse 15, He told them to get the Gospel to the whole world, and then Jesus went up into Heaven. The disciples must have thought, "Wow. He ripped our faces off." Then a few days later, the disciples started sharing the Gospel, and two years later there were 100,000 people that were members of the church at Jerusalem! The Gospel was spread into Samaria and the European areas. We have the Gospel in America today because the disciples got busy.

I am glad to counsel my members who are having problems. However, while I am trying to fix their problems, I am not going to stop the work of the ministry and devote myself to being a marital counselor 168 hours a week. I could do professional marriage counseling the rest of my days, but that is not my calling. My calling is to make sure the Chicago area has the Gospel. We were put on this earth to do the works of God, to glorify God and magnify His name, to manifest the works of God in our life. We have a great world out there. There are 250,000 teenagers in the Chicago area. About 1,000 of them come to our church on Sundays. What about the other 249,000? Parents, while you are trying to figure out your own kids and get them in line, hit the ball and drag the kids along with you and try to help other teenagers who don't know Christ.

Christian colleges are starting all over in the United States competing for the same students. China has 1.3 billion people and no Christian colleges at all. How about if we get those Christian schools going over there, ship those graduates back to America to Hyles-Anderson College, and train some red-hot evangelists to go back to China to win their own people. Let's get some South Koreans going for Christ! Let's get the Filipinos going for Christ! Let's get the New Zealand folk and the Australian people and the Bulgarian people and the Brazilian people and the Peruvian people and the South American people going for Christ! The world is wide open to us!

The world is going to Hell because Christians are wrapped up in their life-size problems and neglecting the works of God. Husband, if you and your wife are having marital problems and you just can't seem to fix her, grab your wife, and say to her, "You don't like me, and I don't like you. But let's go win the world to Christ."

"The world is going to Hell because Christians are wrapped up in their life-size problems and neglecting the works of God."

My wife and I are not happy because we have a "happy bug" that we inherited genetically from our parents. My wife and I are happy because we are in a yoke together pulling the same way. When I see my wife doing her best to please her Saviour, I

The Great Distraction

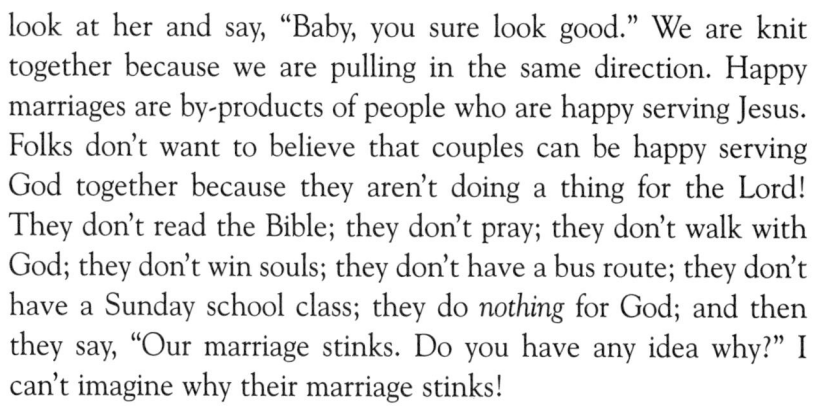

look at her and say, "Baby, you sure look good." We are knit together because we are pulling in the same direction. Happy marriages are by-products of people who are happy serving Jesus. Folks don't want to believe that couples can be happy serving God together because they aren't doing a thing for the Lord! They don't read the Bible; they don't pray; they don't walk with God; they don't win souls; they don't have a bus route; they don't have a Sunday school class; they do *nothing* for God; and then they say, "Our marriage stinks. Do you have any idea why?" I can't imagine why their marriage stinks!

How is your bus route doing? How is your Sunday school class growing? How many converts sit in church because of you and your wife? Most folks want to go to church and complain, "We have life-size problems, and the pastor has to fix them for us." What they need to do is forget about **their** problems and get to work helping others with their problems!

A wife never looks so good as she does when her husband wants to do something great for God, and she says, "Go for it!" A man never looks so good as when he says, "I need you. Follow me. We're going somewhere."

All of us have life-size problems today, and our problems will probably be there tomorrow, too. While the problem's are not going away, get more people saved. Will that fix the problem? I don't know. Jesus did not promise the blind man that he would be healed if he washed in the pool of Siloam. He **was** healed. And no doubt, many other blind people went to the pool of Siloam after hearing of that healing and washed and bathed, but walked away blind. The great secret for an individual to handle and deal with his problems is found in his willingness to obey God and the Word of God.

CHAPTER SEVEN

I Understand It, But I Don't Get It!

"*In Gibeon the Lord appeared to Solomon in a dream by night: and God said, Ask what I shall give thee. And Solomon said, Thou hast shewed unto thy servant David my father great mercy, according as he walked before thee in truth, and in righteousness, and in uprightness of heart with thee; and thou hast kept for him this great kindness, that thou hast given him a son to sit on his throne, as it is this day. And now, O Lord my God, thou hast made thy servant king instead of David my father: and I am but a little child: I know not how to go out or come in. And thy servant is in the midst of thy people which thou hast chosen, a great people, that cannot be numbered nor counted for multitude. Give therefore thy servant an understanding heart to judge thy people, that I may discern between good and bad: for who is able to judge this thy so great a people? And the speech pleased the Lord, that Solomon had asked this thing. And God said unto him, Because thou hast asked this thing, and hast not asked for thyself long life; neither hast asked riches for thyself, nor hast*

> "As long as the Christian has to have his life's problems solved, then God is on constant trial as to whether or not He is good."

104 ❖ Is God Enough for You?

asked the life of thine enemies; but hast asked for thyself understanding to discern judgment; Behold, I have done according to thy words: lo, I have given thee a wise and an understanding heart; so that there was none like thee before thee, neither after thee shall any arise like unto thee." (I Kings 3:5-12)

This is quite a story. God seemed to be waiting to hear what Solomon was going to ask and say. Here's Solomon, a man who is around 40 years old, who is taking command of his father's throne. Solomon has prepared a very careful speech, a prayer to give to God. At the conclusion of Solomon's speech, God is very pleased.

Notice verse 9, "*Give therefore thy servant an understanding heart to judge thy people, that I may discern between good and bad: for who is able to judge this thy so great a people?*"

The implication in this story is that if Solomon had asked for riches, God would have given him riches. If Solomon had asked for long life, God would have given him a long life. In the kindness of God, because God was very pleased with Solomon's request, He threw in all the other benefits on the side. God always gives more than that for which we ask. God is a very generous God.

No doubt, each of us has wondered many times if we were ever to be in a situation such as Solomon's and God were ever to appear to us and say, "I want you to ask Me for anything you want. Don't give Me a laundry list of 15 things you want, but bottom line, list what you want. Tell Me what you want for the rest of your life, and I will give it to you," for what would we ask?

Of course, we know that Solomon's speech pleased the Lord, so I used to think that I would ask for wisdom and an understanding heart. However, that troubled me for a long time. God said that He would give Solomon the exact answer to that for which he asked. Solomon had more understanding than anyone who ever lived. Solomon had more wisdom than anyone who ever lived before or after him. Solomon was world renown for his wisdom and understanding.

Solomon had incredible wisdom and understanding. However, if a person even casually studies the life of Solomon, he would scratch his head and say, "Was Solomon a wise man or a wise guy?" On one side, he wrote the book of Proverbs. Solomon wrote about a man being happy with the wife of his youth. Well, Solomon, the questions is—which one? Solomon had 1,000 women. Solomon did have tremendous wisdom in judging the people. Solomon was tremendous in organizing the people. Solomon had great wisdom in rallying the people to go forward and build a nation. The nations around him sat in awe of Solomon's wisdom. The Queen of Sheba visited Solomon and said, "I've heard about you; but the half has not been told."

Yet, Solomon not only married 1,000 women, but the women he married were outlandish women. Solomon also brought in all their false gods with them. He built each a special house and religious shrines for each. Solomon married many of these women for political reasons to keep peace with the nations, yet he loved all of them. Now, the nation of Israel had a plurality of religions instead of one God. The people's hearts left worshiping Jehovah God, and Solomon actually set up the worst machinery for a government; and as soon as Solomon died, the kingdom split. How could such a wise man do such foolish things? As this passage of Scripture is studied, the problem becomes apparent.

Notice again in verse 9 what Solomon asked, "*Give therefore thy servant an understanding heart to judge thy people....*" Solomon certainly did become a great judge of the people, but somehow in getting all that wisdom and understanding, Solomon missed a very basic principle that many Christians today miss as well.

Is God Enough for You?

In my marriage counseling, sometimes I counsel a couple who just doesn't seem to get it. I once said to a couple, "You two have a problem that is rare. I think you have too much going for you to have a good marriage. Both of you are too smart to have a good marriage. You understand each other too well. You understand you have marriage problems too well. You understand all that I teach too well. **You** grasp the truths I teach better than **I** grasp them sometimes, but you don't get it." There is a difference in the Christian life between understanding it and getting it.

Hundreds of Christians understand the Christian life as well as I do. They have been saved for many years. They have been rooted and grounded in Christian growth. They are well educated and could probably explain theology. They understand all the lessons that have been taught in their Sunday school classes. They know how to win a soul to Christ, and they have won dozens and some even hundreds to Christ. They don't lack understanding and wisdom. They excel in so many areas. They are on the way to becoming ten times better than the world. They dress sharper than the world. They act sharper than the world. They have a good approach to life. Yet, some just don't get it. There are some couples whose marriages have suffered for 15 to 20 years. They have gone to many different counselors. They have read all the books and listened to all the tapes on marriage, and they probably grasp marital truth as well as or better than anybody else; but they don't get it.

> "Christians do not have to understand their problems to fix their problems."

Here is a great principle. Christians do not have to understand their problems to fix their problems. Far too many Christians are waiting to understand the problem before they can fix the problem. If that is what they are waiting for, they will never see their problem fixed.

I Understand It, But...

Solomon had it all. He understood all the problems. Solomon wrote the book on how to deal with life's problems—Proverbs. He wrote the book on what not to do about life's problems—Ecclesiastes. He wrote 3,000 proverbs on how the Christian should live his life; yet, Solomon didn't get it. At the very conclusion of the entire matter, he grasped it when it was too late. Solomon said in Ecclesiastes 12:13, *"Let us hear the conclusion of the whole matter: Fear God, and keep his commandments: for this is the whole duty of man."* That was the end of Solomon's writing before his death.

In those words, I find why Christians do not grow and work. There are very few things that a person uses successfully in life that he understands—for instance, electric lights. We know there is a wall switch that if we turn it on, the lights come on; if we turn it off, the lights go off. If a person is a rescue mission man and he flips the light switch on, the lights will come on. If a fallen woman flips the light switch off, the lights will go off. If a drug addict or an alcoholic turns the light switch on, the lights go on. If a child switches the light switch on, it will cause the lights to go on. An unsaved person can flip that light switch and turn the lights on or off. There is a marvelous principle: I don't have to understand any of it to use it.

Suppose a passenger on an airplane called to the attendant and said, "Before we take off, I want to understand aerodynamics." That passenger will be sitting on that plane until he dies of old age! The truth of the matter is that even if someone could explain aerodynamics to that passenger, there are even many incredibly bright physicists who don't know exactly why an airplane flies. They can tell you it is because the laminar flow creates a low-pressure zone above the wing and a high-pressure zone under the wing; however, the truth of the matter is, they really don't know why it does that. The government has spent one million dollars to analyze why a Frisbee flies. The conclusion is—we don't know why.

There is so much in life we don't understand. When we put the key in the ignition of a car, most of us do not understand how the turning of the key sends electricity from the battery to a starter. Unless a person is a mechanic, he probably doesn't understand how it works. Most people don't even know where the starter is on their car. Explain how the windshield wiper works. Explain how a tire is made. Explain how the engine works.

Ninety-nine percent of that which we do in our lives cannot be explained by us. However, if a person will obey God's natural laws, they will work. Too many people have gotten too smart to become very good Christians. They get to the point where they want to understand Christianity and understand it and understand it; but, the more they understand it, the more they become very good in pointing out or judging other people. The more a Christian judges other people, the less obedient he becomes.

> *"The more a Christian judges other people, the less obedient he becomes."*

At the beginning of his reign, Solomon was the most obedient. The more he focused on understanding, the less obedient he became. Solomon's wisdom increased while his obedience decreased. That divergence from obedience to understanding caused him to get to the point where he did not know how ignorant he really was. Every time I read about Solomon, I cringe because the wisest man in all the world married 1,000 women and allowed them to bring their false gods. Each time I read his life story, I hope that it will be a little different and that Solomon won't do the same foolish things. I want to read Proverbs to him!

Solomon had great wisdom in the account of the two harlots who both had babies and came to him for a decision. (I Kings 3:16-27) The women were living in the same house. One rolled over on her baby and suffocated the baby. When she woke up in the middle of the night and realized her baby was dead, she swapped babies with her friend and gave her friend the dead baby, and she took the live baby. The next morning her friend realized the dead baby in her arms was not her baby. The other woman said, "No, the living baby is my baby." To settle the dispute, they went to Solomon for a decision. When Solomon called for a sword to cut the baby in half to give half to each mother, the biological mother immediately cried, "No! Let her have the baby."

When the true mother of the dead baby said, "That's a good idea," Solomon gave the the baby to the real mother. What wisdom he possessed!

Solomon was so able to discern other people's problems that he was able to judge the mistakes of others and see through the phoniness and hypocrisy of others. If he was so able to judge others, why couldn't he see the right and wrong in himself? Solomon forgot several basic principles.

1. I don't have to understand my problems to fix my problems. If a person says, "I will understand all about marriage before I will get married," that person will die very alone. The married person who says, "I must understand my spouse," will never fix his marriage problems.

The young man who says, "Before I preach, I have to understand the call to preach," will never preach. I have been preaching for 29 years, and I still don't understand the call to preach. I can't explain how God walked into my room on May 6, 1975, and called me to preach. I can't explain it, but I know it happened.

Most of the Christian life cannot be explained. No one can fully explain the Bible. Someone asked Daniel Webster if he read the Bible. He replied "Yes, I do."

The person asked, "Do you understand the Bible?"

"Not much of it," Mr. Webster truthfully answered.

"Does that fact bother you?"

"No," Mr. Webster replied. "It's not the Bible I don't understand that bothers me. It's the Bible I do understand that bothers me."

2. The time spent waiting to understand the problem is time spent disobeying. The child who says, "I must understand my parents before I obey my parents," is a rebel. If the command is given in the Bible and a person understands the command 20 years later, he spent 20 years in rebellion against God. Every moment a Christian spends saying, "I don't get it. I'm going to wait until I understand it," he is saying, "I'm a rebel."

A teenager may say, "I want to understand what's wrong with rock 'n' roll music before I stop listening to it." What if he never understands what is wrong with rock music? What if the preacher never uses the right words that get through to that teenager?

In an appointment with a teenager, he said, "I have heard you preach about the wrongs of rock music. I haven't yet heard one good reason from you that makes sense to me. I don't mean to be disrespectful, but I don't believe that I am obligated to stop listening to my rock music until you or someone else can convince me that it is wrong."

"Suppose you are about to eat rat poison," I suggested. "You have the spoon at your mouth. Suppose I couldn't convince you in understandable terms why it is not good for you to eat that rat poison. Are you going to go ahead and eat it?"

"But I know what's wrong with rat poison," he assured me.

"Explain it to me," I instructed him.

"It's dangerous."

I asked, "What's dangerous about it?"

"It kills rats," he explained.

I asked, "How does it hurt humans?"

"I don't know," he admitted. "Is it bad for you?"

I Understand It, But...

"No," I said sarcastically. "It's very good for you. I would eat the whole box if I were you!"

If Christianity hangs upon logic, then Christianity is a farce. Not one person can make sense of everything about Christianity and the Christian life.

A husband came to me and asked me to talk to his wife about her appearance. He didn't want to put down his foot and tell her she couldn't wear britches, but it bothered him when she did. They came to see me. The wife said, "I'm going to give you a hearing. If you can make sense of it to me, then I'll stop wearing my britches; but I don't think I am obligated to obey you until you make sense."

> "If Christianity hangs upon logic, then Christianity is a farce. Not one person can make sense of everything about Christianity and the Christian life."

"Ma'am, you hit the nail on the head," I agreed. "You're not obligated to obey me at all, but you are obligated to obey your husband. What if I don't make sense of it, what if your husband doesn't make sense of it, but what if your husband doesn't want you to wear britches?"

"I'm not going to obey my husband until I understand my husband," she declared.

I said, "That's the most retarded statement I've ever heard in my life. Do you understand everything about your husband?"

Cynically she said, "Yeah, right!"

"So, you're not going to obey your husband in any area," I concluded. I looked at the husband and said, "Command your wife to go to Disney World with you."

"I'd do that!" she excitedly agreed.

"But you have to pay for it," I shot back.

"No, he's in charge and it's his responsibility."

I said, "It's funny how you are so able to judge your husband's role when it comes to your pleasure or comfort, but you cannot judge your husband's role when it comes to something with which you disagree. You have no problem reminding your husband that he owes your family a vacation every year. You have no problem reminding your husband that you require him to buy school clothing for your children. You have no problem reminding him about your anniversary or Mother's Day or Christmas. You have no problem reminding him about your parents' birthdays. You have no problem reminding him about the Christian school tuition he must pay. You have no problem reminding your husband about the duties he is required to perform, but somehow his duties do not extend to your discomfort! If you are going to judge your husband only on what you understand about your husband, then you have a very limited obedience; and limited obedience is disobedience. Disobedience means your husband is married to a witch because the Bible says, *'For rebellion is as the sin of witchcraft....'* (I Samuel 15:23a) I did not say it; take it up with God!"

If a Christian has to understand what is wrong with rock music before he will stop listening to it, or understand what is wrong with cocaine before he won't sniff it, or understand what is wrong with marijuana before he won't smoke it, or understand what is wrong with premarital intimacy before he stays pure, or understand what's wrong with pornography before he stops looking at, then he is condemning himself to a wasted, unhappy, miserable life.

The staff member who has to understand loyalty before he is loyal is a disloyal rebel. If a child has to understand obedience before he obeys, then he is a rebel. When a Christian says, "God, I'm a Christian, but You have to make me understand everything before I obey You," the time spent between the Christian's understanding and his obeying is time spent in rebellion. How can the

I Understand It, But...

Christian expect God to bless a rebel? God wants to bless each Christian's life. However, there is no verse in the Bible that says God will bless our lives because we understand the commandments. God blesses obedience.

3. God has ordained obedience to be the tool that changes the Christian. There are many things we can understand about the Bible. For those who read and seek to obey the Bible, sometimes we can be amazed with the insight the Bible gives us. Sometimes others will take note of what we say or do and recognize that we are making wise decisions.

However, sometimes it is a marvel that the truths we know and understand don't change us. What changes us is that we obey God. What changes a marriage is that the husband obeys the command, *"Husbands, love your wives."* (Ephesians 5:25a) The Bible never commands a husband to understand his wife. (Even God is not that smart!) However, God does command each husband to love his wife.

I was counseling with a couple, and I said to the wife, "You probably don't even know what a wife is required to do."

"Well, I'm supposed to love my husband," she offered.

I said, "No, the Bible never commands you to love your husband." The Bible commands the wife to sit under a mature, spiritual woman who will teach her how to love her husband, but she is not commanded to love her husband. The Bible commands the wife to obey her husband.

> *"Obedience is the greatest tool because everyone can obey."*

Obedience is the greatest tool because everyone can obey. If a Christian waits until he understands the Bible to read the Bible, he will soon be a non-Bible-reading Christian. None of us will ever fully understand the Bible, but if I have to wait to understand it fully to obey it, then I will never obey one command.

Is God Enough for You?

A Christian's saying, "I have to understand it before I obey it," is utter nonsense. There will never be sufficient understanding for us to become the blessed Christian God wants us to be.

Most new Christians who get baptized do not understand why they got baptized. But they are obedient. A church bulletin once read, "Next month we are having our baptismal classes to prepare for our annual baptism." What was the pastor of that church trying to get those new converts to understand? I wonder if he has that same approach with his children. Does he say to his sons, "Sons, we are going to have the annual grass-cutting ceremony to teach you how to cut grass so that when I say 'cut the grass' you will understand why I want you to cut the grass"? Does he say to his children, "We are going to have our annual bed-making convention so I can teach you why it is important for you to make your beds?" or "We are going to have our annual why-we-wash-our-hands ceremony so you will understand why you should regularly wash your hands? But if you don't understand it, then don't do it."

> "There is no area of life in which we act more foolishly than in the area of obeying God."

There is no area of life in which we act more foolishly than in the area of obeying God. If I say to my kids, "Go wash your hands before supper," I don't expect them to ask me to explain to their understanding why they must wash their hands, but I do expect them to obey.

When my wife is out of town for a few days, do you think I make my bed? Yes, I do, because I was taught to make my bed. Do I understand why I make the bed? No. I still don't understand why a bed has to be made that is going to get unmade again that night. Why go through the ritual of straightening out the sheets? I don't understand, but I make my bed.

The truth of the matter is that most of life's rituals are a big,

I Understand It, But...

boring waste of time. I brush my teeth three or four times a day. Why? I don't know. The dentist says that brushing your teeth prevents cavities. I have a whole mouth of cavities. The dentist lied to me!

Whoever invented shaving ought to have his head shaved! Some men never shave less than twice daily, and sometimes three or four times daily. Most men don't understand why. Why did God give men beards if they are supposed to shave them all the time?

Why do we have grass? How much time do we spend mowing grass? Why?

Most of our lives are spent doing things we don't understand. But somehow in doing things we don't understand, we become better people for doing so because God ordained obedience as a tool of change.

> *"Somehow in doing things we don't understand, we become better people for doing so because God ordained obedience as a tool of change."*

4. **Obedience releases all of God's power.** If a microphone is removed from the microphone cord, there will be problems. Few if any will be able to hear the speaker's voice. A speaker can talk all day into that microphone, but it will do little good. The microphone will not project a voice. It may look good, but it will not project a voice. However, the microphone that is connected to the microphone cord will work for anybody. The Christian who will obey will receive all the benefits of obedience. A Christian may say, "I'm not worthy to plug a microphone into the cord." That doesn't matter. Just obey.

Most people do not understand how a person can talk into a cell phone and another person thousands of miles away hears that voice instantaneously. But all one has to do is obey the principles of the cell phone. One simply has to turn it on and talk.

Those who obey the law will get the benefit. Obey the Book;

It works. Obedience works for everybody. It seems ignorant to us for a person to say, "I won't use a cell phone until I understand it," or "I won't use my computer until I understand it." But the simple truth is that obedience to a principle or truth always garners rewards.

> "*Obedience to a principle or truth always garners rewards.*"

5. It is possible to understand without obeying. Many Christians have a grasp on the Word of God, but the Word of God has never changed their lives at all. There are authors who write books as experts on subjects who don't live by their own teaching. There was a pastor who wrote a book about how to be sure your inner world is strong and not hypocritical. While he was writing the book, he was having an affair. His life collapsed. He lost his marriage. Then he wrote another book about the hypocrite he was while he was writing the first book! In the second book, the author said that he understood the principles about which he wrote in the first book, but he was not obeying them.

A Christian college professor can get up in a college classroom and teach the Bible and teach how to prepare a sermon while at the same time he might be living a hypocritical, immoral, ungodly life. Teenagers can learn biblical principles in their Christian school and go off to Bible college and understand great things. However, if they are not obeying those same principles and truths, they are like the Pharisees whom Jesus said were hypocrites, "*...whited sepulchres...full of dead men's bones....*" (Matthew 23:27)

6. Understanding allows me to help others obey; it does not make me obey. The more a person understands the truth, the more he can help others obey the truth. When I was taking a pilot's training course, my trainer understood much more about flying than I did; therefore, he was able to teach me how to fly. It got to a point one day in my flying when he looked at me and

I Understand It, But...

said, "You are becoming a better pilot than I am. You are a very good pilot. I understand more than you do, so I can still teach you, but you are becoming a better pilot." Many things that instructor taught me I didn't understand. I just did what he told me to do. When I did what he told me to do, my obeying his instructions changed me.

If young people could only understand why they should read the Bible. Some will say, "I read it, but it doesn't change me. I don't understand it." Read the Bible! Try Bible reading and prayer for 50 years. Try decency for the rest of your life. Solomon should have tried living what he taught—to be satisfied with one woman the rest of his life, and then he would have been happy and not brought damnation to the nation of Israel. Solomon wrote the book on how to live when he, through inspiration, penned the book of Proverbs, but he did not live and obey what he wrote.

A husband whose marriage was foundering once told me, "I'm going to tell you what the problem is with America's marriages." I'll be honest; he had a tremendous grasp on the problem.

I listened to him and said, "I don't believe I have ever had a man come to my office with a marital problem with such a grasp of why a marriage is on the rocks."

"I study those things, Pastor," he acknowledged. "I have thought and thought and thought. I know why marriages fail. I even know why I am losing my marriage."

"No, you don't know that," I countered.

"I do too," he asserted. "Let me tell you why." He laid out the reasons point by point.

"You forgot one thing," I noted. "It isn't how much you know; it's what you do. **You** will not obey."

He said, "I suppose you are telling me that I have to love my wife no matter what!"

"No. I'm not telling you that at all," I stated. "God told you that." I brought in his wife and said, "The Bible says, '*Wives, submit yourselves unto your own husbands, as unto the Lord.*' " Then I said to the husband, "Until you love your wife like you would go to Calvary for her," and to the wife, "Until you submit to him like you would submit to Jesus Christ, your marriage is going to stink!"

It is not the lack of understanding that causes problems; it is lack of obedience that causes problems. A Christian can talk and talk and talk and talk and understand and understand, but until he is willing to obey, the truth is **not** going to work. The person who wrote the book on microphones will not be able to use the microphone unless he plugs it into the source of power. God is not impressed with a Christian's knowledge and understanding. He is impressed with the Christian's obedience.

7. **It is possible to teach others to obey while not obeying yourself.** At first, this type of teaching sounds impressive, but as the old adage says, "Actions speak louder than words."

8. **Partial obedience is rebellion.** A child's incomplete obedience is not acceptable to a parent. Our partial obedience to God is no less rebellious to the Heavenly Father.

9. **The need to understand before obeying is mind worship.** There is much idolatry going on in Christianity. Many young adults are making foolish mistakes. They are going to get their own apartments and set their own curfews and live their own lives and be their own man. They are bowing down to a god called their little pea brain! They proudly boast, "I know what is best for me."

When students get in trouble at school, I spend some time with them. I want to find out what they are thinking. What bothers me more than anything is that they think they **"know"** how to get themselves out of trouble. They think they **"know"** what is best for themselves. They don't know anything! They got into trouble because they were disobedient.

I Understand It, But...

Until they are willing to look at their authorities and say, "Sir, I don't know what to do. Would you please tell me?" they cannot be helped. The prodigal son finally came to himself and in so many words said, "Dad, I'm not worthy to be your son. If you'll just tell me how to live, I'll be a slave to you and be happy. Whatever you tell me to do, I'll do." Why didn't he learn that lesson before he left home?

The first thing the military does to new recruits is to shave their heads, tell them to shut up, tell them how to dress and what socks to wear, tell them when to get up and when to go to bed, tell them when to eat and what they can eat, tell them what they can do and when they can do it and how to do it and with whom to do it. The new recruit does not get a vote in the matter. The recruit who walks in and says, "I've read the manual on how you're doing this," will be greeted by, "Shut up! We don't care about your understanding. We just want your obedience."

We have too many sophisticated Christians attending our churches who understand the system, but don't have the obedience to match their understanding.

10. Obedience brings understanding, but understanding does not necessarily bring obedience. If I do obey, it is amazing how I will eventually say, "Well, that's starting to make a little sense." Then I obey some more, and I understand some more. Then 20 years after first obeying, I will say, "I have a grasp of that concept, and I am experiencing the blessings of God!" The person who truly wants to understand must obey first and then understand. The worst way to live is to expect to understand first and then obey.

For those who are graduating from high school, this is the approach they should take at that stage in life. It is the approach I took, and it is the approach that will make a person happy. My dad said, "Go to college."

I asked, "Where?"

"Ask your pastor," Dad instructed.

I asked my pastor, and when he said, "Go to Pillsbury Baptist Bible College," I said, "I don't want to go there." But I obeyed and went. Did I enjoy it? No. Did I understand it? Absolutely not. But the life of obedience has been a life of blessing that is indescribable and unexplainable.

Real happiness cannot be explained. One cannot explain a happy marriage versus an unhappy marriage. One cannot explain the difference between friends who had to do it their way and others who said, "I don't understand what my pastor wants me to do, but I will do it." There have been scores of times when I sat in Brother Hyles' office and had a game plan in my mind of what I felt was the best way to do something, and Brother Hyles would take my game plan and shred it verbally into little tiny pieces and blow it into Never-Never-Land. I wanted to say, "But you don't understand."

One time Brother Hyles said to me, "I bet you think I don't understand, don't you?"

"Well, I guess the thought passes through my mind occasionally," I admitted.

He said, "First of all, I do understand—better than you do. Secondly, it doesn't matter if I do understand or not, this is the way it's going to be."

I said, "I understand that!"

I spoke to a young married man who was struggling with a decision. He said, "The way I look at it…" and I listened to him for a few minutes.

I said, "Son, I really don't care how you look at it. If you want to work for me, you work for me, and we do it my way. Do you understand that?"

"Yes, I understand that," he agreed.

I Understand It, But...

A point comes where a person must stop trying to figure out life and instead start obeying God. The person who walks over to the light switch and says, "I wonder what happens when I switch that switch?" Do the protons chase the neutrons or the electrons chase the protons?" but never flips the switch, will not turn on the lights.

11. Obedience works for everyone. The Christian who gets in the Word of God will have a rich life. The Word of God will straighten out the mind and cleanse the life. I was talking with some of our Reformers Unanimous workers one day. They said that it is amazing how that some of the folks who come to the Reformers Unanimous program, our Bible-based addiction program, can hardly speak because they are so messed up by drugs and alcohol. The worker said, "Sometimes you think there is no hope for those people. But the Word of God starts getting in their brain and starts straightening out all their messes." Reformers Unanimous is not a program whereby people are taught to understand why the program works; we just say, "Do it! And if you'll do it, it will transform your life."

If the Christian will read his Bible, pray, go soul winning, obey the preaching of the Word of God—all the basics of Christianity, he will have a very fulfilled and rewarding life. The Christian who trusts those who have more understanding based on obedience than he has based on experience will be a happier person for it and will receive the blessings of God. Or a person can choose to live his life, waiting to obey until he understands, and then realize he spent wasted years that could have been filled with blessings and happiness.

"The Christian who trusts those who have more understanding based on obedience than he has based on experience will be a happier person for it and will receive the blessings of God."

122 Is God Enough for You?

Maybe the Lord designed life in such a way that we could not possibly figure out every facet. Maybe in His divine plan He purposely sought to test our obedience over our understanding. For in the tests of "blind obedience," the Lord is actually testing our sincere love for Him. "*If ye love me, keep my commandments.*" (John 14:15)

> "In the tests of "blind obedience," the Lord is actually testing our sincere love for Him."